ART & SCIENCE OF

BALANCE

Finding Bliss in Life's 7 Spectrums

ART & SCIENCE OF

BALANCE

Finding Bliss in Life's 7 Spectrums

DR. PANKAJ CHUGH

PRABHAT
PRAKASHAN

Published by
PRABHAT PRAKASHAN PVT. LTD.
4/19 Asaf Ali Road,
New Delhi-110 002 (INDIA)
e-mail: prabhatbooks@gmail.com

ISBN 978-93-5571-662-0
ART & SCIENCE OF BALANCE
by Dr. Pankaj Chugh

Edition
First, 2023

Price
₹ 250 (Rupees Two Hundred Fifty Only)

Printed at
Japan Art, Delhi

Acknowledgements

In the realm of literary creation, I find myself humbled and indebted to the myriad of masters and teachers who have illuminated my path throughout this wondrous journey. To all the extraordinary beings with whom I have had the privilege of engaging and collaborating, regardless of temporal constraints, I extend my heartfelt appreciation. Moreover, I must extend my deepest gratitude to my beloved family, whose unwavering encouragement has propelled me to pen this captivating novelette. May the splendor of balance eternally grace our existence, and may we all bask in the ecstasy it bestows upon our lives.

❑

Contents

Acknowledgements 5

Introduction 9

1. **Survival:** Red Spectrum 17

2. **Self-Worth:** Yellow Spectrum 33

3. **Self Confidence:** Orange Spectrum 44

4. **Empathy:** Green Spectrum 55

5. **Self-Expression:** Blue Spectrum 66

6. **Self-Knowledge:** Indigo Spectrum 78

7. **Spirituality:** Violet Spectrum 90

7 Pearl Club 101

Rahul & Chairman 109

Introduction

Friday morning dawned with an electric energy at Media Global, as the anticipation for the grand media award event at the city's illustrious amphitheater hung in the air. Rahul, the esteemed CEO of Media Global, found himself amongst the favorite nominees for the coveted Best CEO accolade. The atmosphere was brimming with optimism and hope as the Media Global team eagerly awaited Rahul's triumphant moment, even going so far as to prepare a heartfelt speech in anticipation of his impending victory. Rahul's indelible mark on Media Global' s astounding growth over the past five years had been nothing short of extraordinary. Driven by an unwavering passion for his craft and an unwavering commitment to excellence, he took great pride in his remarkable achievements.

Success had become second nature to him, and he carried an unshakeable certainty that tonight's award would be another feather in his illustrious cap.

Rahul summoned his team to coordinate with his wife, Seema, for the logistics of attending the event. Seema, a skilled freelancer with a degree in computer engineering from a renowned university, shared the news with their daughter, Ayesha, that they needed to gather at Rahul's office by 6:30 pm. From there, they would join Rahul and other esteemed company executives on their way to the grand amphitheater. Ayesha felt a twinge of disappointment, yearning for a shared departure from their home instead. Seema, ever the pillar of support, lifted Ayesha's spirits, explaining that her father had an important board meeting earlier in the day, necessitating their presence at his workplace.

Amidst the bustling energy at Media Global, with the team preparing fervently for the upcoming event, the senior executives found themselves preoccupied with the annual board meeting scheduled for the afternoon. Rahul, accompanied by the Chief Marketing Officer and the Chief Financial Officer, entered the conference room, aligning on crucial matters before the pivotal gathering. The Chairman and seven other directors directed their attention to Rahul, urging him to commence the proceedings. In his opening statement, Rahul highlighted the company's nominations in three esteemed categories for the evening's event. He emphasized these nominations as rays of hope that would rejuvenate the business and attract new clientele. Over the past year, Media Global had experienced setbacks, losing three significant accounts that had left a profound impact on both the company's reputation and financial standing. Concerned directors sought answers, perceiving these losses as early warnings and indicators of potential shortcomings in the company's client engagement processes. In response, Rahul attributed the losses to aggressive commercial terms employed by their competitors. He confidently declared that with tonight's award, Media Global would regain its standing, attracting fresh clients. He proudly announced the company's nomination in the AI Solutions category, expressing almost certainty of securing the award.

The board ultimately approved the financials, albeit with a 70% reduction in dividends for the shareholders. The Chairman, intrigued by Rahul's unwavering focus on awards as a measure of the company's future success, questioned the implications if Media Global failed to secure any accolades that evening. He suggested that the team gather, engage in introspection, and reevaluate their processes to exceed clients' expectations. Unyielding in his belief that the company was on the right path, Rahul made a bold proclamation to prove his point: if Media Global failed to secure any of the three awards, he would step down as CEO. The room fell into stunned silence, with the Chairman breaking the spell by acknowledging Rahul's personal commitment. He accepted Rahul's conditional resignation on behalf of the board, honoring the conviction that had driven the CEO to make such a daring statement.

Rahul's declaration left the CMO and CFO astounded. After the board meeting concluded, they approached him, seeking clarification on his decision. Rahul, brimming with overconfidence, reassured them not to worry and to prepare for the evening's celebrations. He had no regrets, firmly believing that as a leader, he had to stand by his convictions, and he promptly immersed himself in other tasks.

As evening descended, the core team of Media Global departed the office, and Seema inquired about the board meeting. Rahul assured her it had gone well, and as expected, traffic snarls slowed their progress towards the amphitheater. Finally, around 7:50 pm, they arrived at the venue, just in the nick of time. The ceremony commenced promptly at 8, featuring a celebrity anchor flown in specifically for the occasion. After the introduction and expressions of gratitude to the sponsors, the guest of honor was invited to inaugurate the award ceremony. Mr. Siddharth, fondly known as Guru Ji, rose gracefully, acknowledging the immense crowd with a respectful bow before stepping up to the podium. He expressed his humility at being chosen for such an auspicious moment, offering a concise and profound message to the companies and intellectuals in the media industry. Guru Ji implored them to present perspectives across the entire spectrum of life's rainbow, believing it to be a profound service to society, opening doors to values often left unexplored. With that, he declared the award ceremony officially open, surprising the anchor with his brevity. Intrigued, she approached Guru Ji, seeking clarification on his reference to life's rainbow. In response, Guru Ji chuckled and invited her to their rainbow forest, where self-discovery awaited.

The event unfolded with mesmerizing folk dances from the region, culminating in the highly anticipated awards. The first category,

"AI Solutions," held great promise for Media Global, yet a start-up walked away with the coveted accolade. The disappointment weighed heavily on Rahul and his team. As other awards were bestowed, the time arrived for the "Best Media Company" category. To their dismay, New Age Solutions claimed the prize, attributed to their remarkable threefold growth in the current year. A profound silence enveloped the Media Global team, and Seema noticed the beads of perspiration forming on Rahul's forehead. The usually confident CEO had turned into a statue, his expressionless gaze betraying his inner turmoil. Suddenly, an overwhelming unease washed over Rahul as he remembered his conditional resignation. As the award ceremony drew to a close, the announcement for the best CEO award loomed before him, intensifying his anxiety. Finally, the award was bestowed upon another recipient, and Rahul struggled to regain control over his emotions. He couldn't fathom that his company had failed to secure a single award, an unprecedented occurrence in the past five years. The drive back home was filled with an oppressive silence that persisted until they reached their destination.

Rahul requested Seema and Ayesha to give him some space, needing time alone to reflect. He sank into a chair, consumed by thoughts of the events that had unfolded, with the weight of his conditional resignation bearing down on him. A profound sense of despondency overwhelmed him, prompting him to seek solace in a few drinks in the hope of finding sleep. The next morning, he instinctively reached for his mobile phone, but to his surprise, no messages awaited him. The bitter truth of "Success has many fathers, and failure has none" resounded within him. In the afternoon, David, a manager at an NGO and Rahul's former university batchmate, called unexpectedly. Having read about the media award event in the newspaper and the absence of awards for Rahul's company, David felt compelled to reach out and invite him for a coffee. Sensing Rahul's mood, he assured him that there was no pressure to meet but expressed pride in Rahul's past achievements. Rahul agreed, suggesting they meet in the evening at the same location.

As the sun began to set, casting a warm glow over the peaceful café nestled away from the chaos of the city, Rahul and David finally reunited. The aroma of freshly brewed coffee filled the air, creating an atmosphere of comfort and tranquility.

With gratitude in his heart, Rahul expressed his appreciation for David's invitation and the opportunity to share his burden. Overwhelmed by sadness and frustration, he confided in David, revealing his decision to quit his job and the uncertainty that now enveloped his future. Seeking solace, Rahul turned to his friend, yearning to understand the secret behind David's unwavering happiness and remarkable state of bliss.

Puzzled yet intrigued, Rahul questioned David about his unwavering empathy and care, even in the face of his own failures. How could David radiate such peace and contentment, despite the distance that separated him from his family in the United States? David's smile spoke volumes as he replied, his voice tinged with wisdom.

"Rahul, my friend, I attribute my serenity to a concept known as the massive transformative purpose (MTP). It guides and empowers me in every action I take. I owe a debt of gratitude to Guru Ji and the enchanting rainbow forest, where I discovered a unique perspective, one that allows me to witness life's myriad colors."

A memory flickered in Rahul's mind, recalling the presence of Guru Ji at the recent event. In awe, Rahul shared his encounter, noting the few words spoken by the enigmatic guest of honor. David nodded in agreement, affirming Guru Ji's role in fostering self- introspection, a remarkable journey of self-discovery.

Intrigued by David's profound transformation, Rahul expressed his interest in meeting Guru Ji and delving deeper into this mysterious process. Sensing Rahul's curiosity, David offered a gentle suggestion, encouraging him to embark on a personal exploration. "Take one week for yourself, Rahul," he proposed. "Discover the process on your own terms. Perception is projection, and I would rather not influence your experience with my own interpretation. If you're genuinely interested, I can secure a slot for you. The best part? It's free of charge. You only need to manage your meals and refreshments. You'll be assigned to a small group of three other individuals. Sometimes, taking a break and realigning ourselves with our massive transformative purpose can recalibrate our future course."

Without hesitation, Rahul's eyes gleamed with anticipation as he wholeheartedly accepted David's offer. Eager to enroll in the upcoming program, he requested David's assistance in securing a spot for him, a stepping stone toward discovering his own transformative purpose.

❑

1
Survival
Red Spectrum

"It is not the strongest of the species that survive, nor the most intelligent, but the one most responsive to change"

– Charles Darwin

In the early morning hours, Rahul rose from his slumber, greeted by the anticipation of embarking on a transformative voyage. Having committed to a seven-day sojourn at the enchanting Rainbow Forest, he meticulously inspected his belongings, ensuring nothing essential was left behind. Prompt and punctual, he arrived at his destination, only to find his companion, David, awaiting his arrival, had graciously volunteered to assist Rahul in acquainting himself with the program's fundamental procedures, as well as introduce him to the esteemed staff and the enigmatic Guru Ji.

Completing the necessary formalities, Rahul was assigned a cottage nestled amidst the vibrant expanse. "Allow me to carry your burdens to the abode," David offered, his helpful spirit shining through. As they ventured closer to the humble dwelling, Rahul couldn't help but notice the cottage's rustic charm, resembling a quaint hut adorned with blossoming foliage. Crossing the threshold, he discovered a surprising absence of conventional furnishings—a bed, table, and chair were nowhere to be found. Instead, a simple mattress lay upon the pristine floor, accompanied by the necessities of a modest attached washroom.

Curiosity tugged at Rahul's thoughts, compelling him to inquire about the absence of modern amenities. Turning to David, he questioned the conspicuous lack of a television or an air conditioner. A warm smile danced across David's face as he responded, his words carrying profound wisdom, "Welcome, dear friend, to a journey of self-discovery." With a gentle invitation, he suggested they quench their thirst with a refreshing glass of lemon water before the introduction session with Guru Ji.

Curiosity piqued; Rahul posed a query to David regarding his involvement in the forthcoming event. David's eyes sparkled with sincerity as he revealed, "I shall depart after attending the session, reuniting with you on the eighth morning. I eagerly await the opportunity to hear of your profound insights and bask in the wisdom gained during your introspective journey."

Within the expansive common hall, a convergence of approximately 80 individuals marked the beginning of the weekly program. As their collective presence filled the space, anticipation hummed in the air. At the heart of it all, Guru Ji sat humbly on the floor, exuding an aura of anticipation, as if eagerly awaiting the arrival of each participant.

"Thank you," Guru Ji began, his voice carrying a serene resonance that commanded attention, "for embarking on this profound journey of self-discovery. Welcome to the sacred realm of Rainbow Forest. Just as a rainbow manifest through seven vibrant hues, each possessing its own significance, our philosophy resonates with the belief that life itself comprises seven distinct spectrums. Yet, as humans, we often find ourselves entrenched in a mere one or two spectrums, inadvertently overlooking the opportunity to embrace the full spectrum of existence."

With utmost humility, Guru Ji introduced himself, referring to himself as a mere student of life. He expressed his eagerness to learn and grow alongside his attendees, acknowledging the invaluable contribution they would make to his own evolution. Assuredly, he revealed that he and his team of devoted souls were present to guide and facilitate their inner voyage of self-discovery, willingly sharing their own wisdom garnered from their unique journeys. To optimize effective communication and foster intimacy, the gathering was divided into smaller groups of four individuals, each group assigned a dedicated team mentor.

As a token of respect for the harmonious flow of the program, Guru Ji emphasized the importance of adhering to the rules and regulations set forth within this sanctuary. It was not only for the individual's benefit but also for the collective well-being of all present. Entrusting their electronic gadgets to the team mentors, participants were granted a mere half-hour window of accessibility, occurring between 6:00 PM and 6:30 PM.

Setting the tone for the days to come, Guru Ji revealed that the sequence would follow the hues of the rainbow- ROYGBIV, commencing with the exploration of the vibrant red color on this auspicious day. Tomorrow, the focus would shift to the enchanting orange, and so the journey would continue. With genuine warmth, he extended his wishes of good fortune, invoking a heartfelt blessing upon all beings in the universe, "May their path be illuminated with happiness and contentment."

In the enchanting realm of Rainbow Forest, Gopal Ji assumed the role of team mentor for Rahul's group, accompanied by the vibrant individuals Natasha, Simon, and Samantha. Inviting them to find their seats, Gopal Ji initiated the process by urging each member to share a brief introduction. Setting an example, he commenced;

"My name is Gopal Sharma, and I am fortunate enough to serve within the sanctuary of Rainbow Forest. Seven years ago, I, too, embarked on this transformative journey as an attendee, back when I held the prestigious position of Chief Technology Officer in one of America's esteemed Fortune 100 companies. Now, I stand before you as a guide and facilitator, committed to steering our discussions within a framework that will yield collective growth. Above all, it brings me immense joy to be of service to you all."

Natasha gracefully stepped forward, revealing her identity as a fashion designer with a flourishing business consisting of seven boutiques scattered across the state. Additionally, she proudly shared that her brand had expanded nationwide, boasting a network of 30 franchised outlets. Amidst the triumphs, she confided in her fellow journeyers that she carried the weight of a recent divorce, seeking solace and rediscovering her purpose amidst the complexities of life.

Next, Simon took center stage, introducing himself as an insurance agent. With an air of contentment, he expressed genuine satisfaction in his profession, strongly believing that he enriched the lives of his valued clients. Radiating warmth, Simon lovingly spoke of his cherished family—a devoted wife and two beautiful children.

As his gaze pierced the horizon of possibility, he harbored an ardent desire to delve into the mystical realms of spirituality, hoping to unveil profound truths along this sacred pilgrimage.

With a graceful presence, Samantha stepped forward, revealing her vocation as a professor at a prestigious college. As an accomplished author of three finance-related books, she possessed an impressive intellectual acumen. Yet, beneath the veneer of success, Samantha admitted to carrying a burdensome trait—her tendency to be excessively judgmental. It was her heartfelt mission within the sanctuary of Rainbow Forest to transcend this self-imposed limitation, emerging as a more compassionate and open-minded individual.

Lastly, Rahul rose from his seat, radiating a sense of intrigue and uncertainty. Formerly occupying the prestigious position of CEO at Media Global, his journey to this ethereal haven had been guided by a dear friend. Confessing his current state of bewilderment, he candidly confessed, "I find myself in a state of cluelessness at this juncture, yearning to unravel the enigma that lies within."

Within this group of seekers, a fabric of aspirations and yearnings had been woven, each thread seeking illumination amidst the enchantment of Rainbow Forest. Little did they know that their paths would intertwine, their stories converging in a dance of self-discovery and profound transformation.

Gopal Ji, a man of great wisdom and intrigue, let me have your opinion when you see red color. I beseech you to articulate your thoughts, be they but a few words, and let them dance upon our eager ears."

The members of the group exchanged glances, pondering the question posed to them. Slowly, words began to escape their lips, each carrying its own weight of significance. "Blood," one voice whispered, evoking images of life's vitality. "Danger," another cautioned, warning of perils that lay in wait. "Sale," a shrewd observer chimed in, recognizing the allure of commerce. "Stop," echoed a voice, heralding the notion of control. And so, it went on, a tapestry of responses that revealed the diverse facets of their perceptions.

Seizing the thread of their discourse, Gopal Ji stepped forward, his eyes gleaming with wisdom. "Ah, my dear companions," he declared, his voice now a melodic cadence, "let us delve deeper into the enigmatic realms of red. Within its alluring embrace, we find the very essence of survival." The group leaned in, captivated by his words, as he continued to unveil his thoughts.

"As I speak of survival," he expounded, "I refer to the innate instinct that compels us to forge a path of financial security. It is a beacon that guides us, entwined with the safeguarding of our very lives. For the tender souls of youth, it manifests as the yearning for physical safety. In adolescence, it takes the form of an unwavering pursuit of career security. As we venture into the realms of maturity, it morphs into the embodiment of professional self-esteem. And as the circle of life completes its cycle, it returns to its primal manifestation—physical safety once more."

His words hung in the air, laden with introspection and contemplation. Gopal Ji, ever the seeker of truth, reminded his listeners, "Let us not be quick to pass judgment upon the nature of this red spectrum. Instead, let us embrace the profound understanding that I, too, find myself intertwined within its overpowering glow. The purpose lies not in labeling, but in cultivating an awareness that allows our consciousness to serve as our guide, for it is all but a divine arrangement."

In the midst of their profound discussion, Rahul's voice reverberated with a sense of self-realization. "Indeed," he confessed, his words laced with a tinge of vulnerability, "I find myself deeply entwined within this all-encompassing spectrum. It seems that many of my actions and decisions bear the imprint of its influence. While

I cannot claim acquaintance with the other realms just yet, I have come to recognize that survival, security, and safety have shaped my very existence. Could it be that I have become ensnared within the confines of this spectrum?"

Gopal Ji, the sage among them, extended a comforting hand and offered solace to Rahul's weary soul. "Fear not, my dear friend," he reassured, his voice a gentle caress.

"It is premature to draw such definitive conclusions. Let us lend an ear to the wisdom that awaits us."

Simon, with a voice tinged by quiet introspection, interjected, sharing his own sentiments. "Survival, without a doubt, forms the foundation of our existence," he pondered aloud. "In this regard, I find myself aligning with this very spectrum. However, I am not consumed by its weight, for a whisper within me reminds me of the transient nature of all things. 'Why worry,' it implores, 'when everything is but temporary?'"

Eager to contribute her insights, Samantha gracefully stepped forward. Her words flowed like a gentle stream, carrying the weight of universal truth. "Within each and every one of us," she proclaimed, "This spectrum finds resonance. It speaks to the primal urge for survival, manifesting as the necessity to meet our daily needs and forge a life aligned with our aspirations. It is an inherent part of the human experience, binding us all together."

In contrast to the prevailing sentiments, Natasha unveiled a different perspective, her voice filled with a newfound confidence born of entrepreneurial endeavors. "In the early stages of my journey as an entrepreneur," she divulged, "I found myself immersed in this spectrum, a staggering 90% governed by thoughts of survival. However, as my brand flourished and acquired its own equity, the shackles of safety began to loosen their grip. Now, I am infused with a sense of audacious self-assurance, no longer overwhelmed by the notion of mere security."

The group, swayed by the weight of their individual experiences, turned their gaze towards Gopal Ji, seeking his wise judgment. Their eyes pleaded for a verdict, a definitive answer as to who among them was right. With a gentle smile, Gopal Ji shook his head, dismissing the notion of such rigid dualities.

"Dear friends," he began, his voice carrying a soothing cadence, "let us liberate ourselves from the confines of right and wrong, good and bad. Life, you see, is a kaleidoscope of perspectives, each one unique and worthy of consideration. Instead, let us embrace the profound truth encapsulated within the power statement—'Perception is Projection.'" And so, with newfound awareness and gratitude, the group embraced the delicate dance of perception, understanding that within this intricate interplay lay the essence of their shared journey.

Once the group reconvened post lunch, the mentor posed a question that pierced through the fabric of their thoughts. "Imagine," he proposed, his words pregnant with contemplation, "that a loved one approaches you, their heart burdened with the weight of survival and security. How would you respond? How would you ease their troubled spirits?"

Natasha, her voice brimming with wisdom acquired through observation, was the first to offer her insights. “In such moments,” she began, her words gentle yet resolute, “I would remind them of the divine arrangements that govern our existence. Even the humble pigeons, devoid of formal education, find sustenance provided for them each morning. There exists a divine network of interconnectedness, that ensures the co-existence of all beings.”

Rahul, his pragmatic nature shining through, shared his approach. “If someone dear to me confided their insecurities,” he reflected, “I would strive to understand the roots of their fears and offer support. Together, we would craft a plan to overcome those hurdles, for having a plan in place can instill a sense of assurance and control.”

Simon, burdened with a real-life scenario involving his wife’s financial anxieties, poured his heart out. “In my own experience,” he admitted, “I have faced this very situation with my wife. I reassure her that I am putting forth my best efforts, and I remind her that there are other aspects of life that hold immense value. I encourage her to find solace in the love and unity that our family shares. After all, happiness and security extend far beyond monetary measures.”

Samantha, usually a pillar of poise, found herself grappling with uncertainty. She hesitated; her voice filled with a raw vulnerability.

"As I listened to my fellow companions," she confessed, "I couldn't help but question my own capacity to guide others. Would I, like a blind person leading another blind soul, offer any true assistance? I find myself entangled within my own spectrum, yearning to know myself fully, so that I may break free from its confines."

Gopal Ji, his presence radiating with an otherworldly serenity, raised a hand to halt the eager questions that danced upon the lips of the group. "Before you inquire about my course of action," he began "I would gently coax them," he continued, his voice infused with the whisper of ancient secrets, "to reflect upon the treasures concealed within the folds of their existence. To peel back the layers of their perception and behold the overlooked blessings that lie within. It is through this introspective gaze that the divine renewable energy awakens—a force known as 'Gratitude.'"

The room became hushed, as the weight of Gopal Ji's words settled upon the hearts of his listeners. In his vision, the seeds of gratitude would be sown, their growth intertwined with the blossoming of a remarkable attitude. For gratitude held the power to illuminate even the darkest corners of existence, revealing the hidden joys and instilling a sense of wonder.

The group, once burdened by questions and uncertainties, now embarked on a transformative journey, guided by the notion that life was not a single path, but a tapestry of infinite dimensions. And within this vast expanse, the seeds of gratitude took root, unleashing a cascade of blessings upon the seeker's soul.

"Today being the first lot of time went in pre-requisites," the mentor spoke with a sagacity that stirred the air. "I propose we engage in a tranquil interlude, embracing the art of meditation before embarking on a collective voyage with the revered Guru ji. Allow yourselves to immerse in the gentle rhythm of your breath, and let your awareness unfurl like a delicate blossom. Observe, dear ones, without the weight of judgment or the need for alteration. Simply observe, the existence weaves its intricate patterns before your eyes."

In the realm of our unfolding narrative, the afterglow of meditation drew the fragmented groups together once more, their footsteps echoing through the hallowed common hall. A sacred air enveloped the space, as Guru Ji, the beacon of wisdom, awaited their arrival. With an aura that commanded reverence, he inquired about their inner sojourns, seeking glimpses into the labyrinth of their minds.

Silence lingered in the wake of his query, like whispers stifled by the weight of introspection. Then, from the depths of the hushed assembly, a solitary voice emerged, timid yet resolute, confessing, "Amidst the ethereal dance of breath, my mind eluded my grasp, drifting like an untamed current. Its restless tendrils, craving to explore every avenue, impeded my focus." A chorus of agreement followed suit, resonating with shared struggles and acknowledging the trepidation that gripped their souls. Some, too, confessed to lingering in anticipation, yearning for the embrace of an ending.

A serene smile graced the countenance of Guru Ji, a beacon of solace amid the storm of their inner turmoil. “Fear not,” he reassured them, his voice as mellifluous as a soothing melody. “For within the vast wilderness of our minds resides a capricious monkey, leaping from branch to branch, perpetually enthralled by the allure of novelty. Such is the paradoxical blessing bestowed upon us. Yet, should this mischievous simian become fixated on a solitary branch, our journey becomes fraught with challenges.” Remember your first attempt to ride a bicycle, then how you mastered it over time. You all will learn to be observant with practice and consistent efforts. From tomorrow we would be having two meditation sessions first one in the morning to start with and the second one just before our gathering here in evening.

His words resonated deep within the hearts of his listeners; a hidden message veiled beneath the veil of levity. “In jest, yet with profound truth,” he continued, “we must learn to tame this playful monkey within us. Meditation, dear companions, serves as our guiding light, enabling us to steer the course of our minds, rather than succumbing to its whimsical choreography. To become observers, detached yet discerning, is a precious virtue to cultivate upon our collective voyage.”

Listen closely, my dear friends, for I am about to unveil the enigmatic allure of the red spectrum. Ah, yes, I can sense your eagerness to hear my perspective on this matter. Throughout our lives, we have all encountered varied interpretations, each unique in its own right. Let us embark on this journey together, starting with the red spectrum that serves as our default, ingrained within the depths of our human existence. Survival, a primal instinct, drives us relentlessly, compelling us to tread upon this spectrum. Yet, let us not forget that a mere dwelling within its confines can upset the delicate equilibrium of life.

We must meticulously plan our endeavors, pursuing them with unwavering sincerity. However, we must also acknowledge that the assurance of favorable outcomes is but a consequence of numerous intertwining factors. There exists a grander divine arrangement for each and every one of us, and the sooner we awaken to this realization, the richer our lives shall be.

Consider the profound bond between a child and its mother, an emotional tether that persists even after the severing of the umbilical cord at birth. Yet, my friends, I implore you, do not allow yourselves to become ensnared by any tether. In the realm of the professional life's be it job or business, I have witnessed individuals unknowingly bound by an intangible umbilical cord. It is this invisible yet very strong connect to our survival ecosystem that limits the freedom to traverse the vibrant array of life's other spectrums impeded. Such is the consequence of investing excessive time within this realm, succumbing to a subconscious attachment that restricts their passage across the beautiful rainbow of existence.

I do not advocate for a reckless abandonment of one's duties; rather, my purpose is to beckon your attention towards the intangible thread that connects us all to our ecosystem of survival, a thread often overlooked by the masses. Survival, dear all, extends far beyond mere financial considerations; it encompasses the intricacies of social standing, personal pride, and the very essence of our self-identity.

Yet, as you embark upon this profound journey, a revelation awaits— the splendor of alternative spectrums. Each spectrum holds profound significance in our lives, and it behooves us to recognize that we need not be overwhelmed by any one of them. For, you see, the true essence lies in striking a harmonious balance, for excess in any realm can prove detrimental to our well-being.

As the day draws to a close, I implore each and every one of you to find solace in tranquility, embracing the profound wisdom that today has bestowed upon you. I am well aware that this day has been unlike any other, a departure from the ordinary rhythms of your existence. Allow this novelty to wash over you, as you prepare to embark upon a sacred voyage of self-discovery. See you tomorrow morning at the meditation hall.

❑

2
Self-Worth
Yellow Spectrum

"Respect yourself and others will respect you"

- Confucius

In the serene abode of contemplation, bathed in the ethereal light of dawn, Gopal Ji's team arrived at the sacred meditation hall, their presence timely and deliberate. The air thickened with anticipation as the mystic luminary, Guru Ji, graced the stage with his enigmatic presence.

"Today," he began, his words "Direct your unwavering focus to the rhythm of your breath, dear seekers of truth. Sense its gentle ebb and flow, and let your consciousness intertwine with the temperature it bears. And should your restless mind wander astray, fret not, for it is the nature of the mind to wander. Simply persevere, gently guiding it back to the purpose you seek to unfold within."

Post meditation session, with a gentle yet commanding presence, Guru Ji elucidated, his voice carrying the weight of an ancient sage. "Within the depths of your very being lies the essence of self-worth associated with orange spectrum," he revealed, his words resonating with an ineffable truth. "Consider the reverence you hold for yourself; the respect you believe you are deserving of. Reflect upon the intrinsic value that dwells within your being, that which you wish others to recognize and honor." "In doing so, a deeper understanding of this orange spectrum shall unveil itself before you. Understand that this journey transcends material wealth; it transcends the ephemeral confines of mere monetary value."

In the realm of self-discovery, Guru Ji proclaimed, his voice an incantation of empowerment. "For within the sacred chambers of self-respect lies the genesis of your journey along this orange spectrum. It is the cornerstone upon which the tapestry of your self- worth unfurls." Another important aspect is how much you value yourself; do you respect yourself to the extent you deserve to be respected.

Within the sanctum of your team discussions, a differentiation between what you deserve and what you desire as self-worth will unfold. "Understand, my beloved seekers, that self-worth transcends mere wishes," Guru Ji elucidated, his words flowing like a benevolent river. "It is the embodiment of your very being, a resolute manifestation of your divine essence. Through this transformation, you shall command the respect you so rightfully deserve."

With each revelation, the disciples recognized that this journey was not one of whimsical desires but a profound transformation of their inner landscape. In that sacred space, the disciples discovered the art of honoring their own existence, of cherishing the unique rainbow of their being.

As the resonant echoes of Guru Ji's profound discourse gradually subsided, Gopal Ji extended a gentle wave to his team, a silent invitation for them to gather in contemplation. "Dear companions," he spoke with a warmth that mirrored the morning sun, "would you be inclined to share your thoughts, to embark upon a collective voyage of exchange?" Their responses echoed as a harmonious chorus, their desire for introspection unanimously voiced. "We yearn for a moment of solitude, an hour perhaps, to delve deep into the chambers of our souls," they expressed in unison.

A knowing smile danced upon Gopal Ji's lips as he recognized the significance of their request. "Indeed," he acknowledged, "the sacred sanctum of self-reflection requires time and space. Your yearning for introspection is honored."

Yet, ever the guiding beacon, Gopal Ji ventured to offer a compass for their inner odyssey. "As you traverse the complexities of self-worth," he proposed, his voice laced with wisdom, "consider four distinct dimensions that shape your existence. Focus upon the realms of Profession, Family, Friends, and Society, and contemplate your self-worth from each unique perspective." He urged them to embark upon this introspective journey with an independent gaze, viewing their worth through the prism of these four realms.

As the hour of introspection came to its gentle close, a stirring of courage welled within Simon's soul. Simon began, his words tinged with vulnerability, "I am blessed with an abundance of love and respect within my family's embrace. In the realm of my profession, my clients extend to me a measure of respect that I have strived to earn. Yet, as I peer into the realm of friendship, I find myself adrift in a sea of uncertainty, lacking the very essence that binds hearts." "When it comes to society," he confessed, his voice tinged with introspection, "I find myself unable to pass judgment.

Samantha's voice emerged, radiant with a newfound sense of contentment. "I have discovered a sense of self-worth that fills me with boundless satisfaction." "From the lens of family, dear companions," Samantha expressed, her voice tinged with gratitude, "I am truly blessed. "Within the realm of my work and friends," she revealed, her words shimmering with a quiet pride, "I am met with reverence and esteem." "Ah, my friends," she whispered, her voice laced with a sense of purpose, "in the realm of society, I find my life adorned with the hues of gratitude and fulfillment. Through my selfless act of teaching finance and accounts, I have been graced with a profound respect from the world around me."

Within the sacred circle of introspection, Natasha's voice emerged, laced with a vulnerability that mirrored the delicate petals of a blossoming flower. "Amidst the complex paths of my existence," Natasha confessed, her voice tinged with a bittersweet honesty, "I find myself traversing a path strewn with judgments within the realm of family. Yet, dear companions, I take solace in the shimmering light of respect that bathes my professional endeavors and nourishes my friendships." "Ah, the enigma of society," she pondered, her voice tinged with a curious wonder. "In this realm, my emotions remain a maze that I have yet to fully comprehend. The complexities of societal perceptions elude my understanding, leaving me yearning for clarity."

"Amidst the network of my existence," Rahul began, his voice a mixture of introspection and contemplation, "I find myself standing at the crossroads of uncertainty. Do I bask in the respect bestowed upon me within the realms of my profession and friendships, or does my position within the corporate world cast an uncertain shadow upon their intentions?" "Ah, my dear family," he confessed, his voice laced with a tinge of remorse, "I believe their reverence embraces me, but alas, I must confess that I have not nurtured the bonds of kinship as

I should. The fleeting nature of time has denied me the opportunity to truly feel the depths of their respect." "As I gaze upon the web of society," he revealed, his voice infused with a solemn tone, "I must concede that I do not believe I deserve the respect bestowed upon me. The accolades and accomplishments I possess, they are solely for my own gain or that of the organizations I serve."

A gentle smile graced Gopal Ji's lips, illuminating the room as he extended his heartfelt congratulations to the team. "In the intricate coil of existence," he began, his words a symphony of guidance and insight, "respect assumes two forms, each bestowed upon us by different means. There are those who effortlessly command respect, their aura forged by the weight of their achievements. And then there are those who diligently earn it, their actions and deeds weaving the fabric of reverence."

Respect, he proclaimed, was the bedrock upon which trust and love found their footing. "But here lies the crux, dear friends," he said, his voice carrying the weight of revelation. "How we conduct ourselves, how we traverse the journey of life, determines the respect we earn. It is through the humble acts of giving back, sharing, and caring that the seeds of respect take root within us."

As Gopal Ji's wisdom settled upon the hearts of the team, a sense of purpose washed over them. They yearned to embrace the path of earning respect, to cultivate the seeds of reverence through selfless acts and heartfelt kindness. "I implore you to embark upon a journey of self-reflection. Close your eyes and envision the ideal image of your self-worth, for within that vision lies the blueprint for your destiny. And then, armed with this clarity, craft a do-list, a sacred compilation of actions that will bring you closer to the embodiment of your ideal self."

The room pulsated with a newfound energy, as the seekers embraced the power of intention. They understood that this simple act of introspection held the key to unlocking their true potential. As the sun dipped below the horizon, casting a warm golden glow upon the world, the seekers gathered once again, drawn to the sacred space of meditation.

And when the final strains of meditation caressed their being, a hush settled upon the room. They knew that the time had come to listen, to absorb the pearls of wisdom that Guru Ji would bestow upon them. With bated breath and hearts open, they prepared themselves to receive his key takeaway, ready to embrace the transformative insights that awaited them.

With a voice that commanded attention and a demeanor steeped in wisdom, Guru Ji addressed the eager gathering. The air crackled with anticipation as his words floated through the space, settling upon the hearts of the seekers like gentle whispers of enlightenment.

"Dear seekers," "in addition to the profound introspection and the guidance bestowed upon you by your mentors, I feel compelled to share a story that may have graced your ears before. But fear not, for within the folds of familiarity lies the power to reshape your perspective, offering a new lens through which to view the prism of the four dimensions."

In the depths of a cozy study, a father and his son shared a profound moment, their connection bridging the gap of generations. "Son," the father spoke with a voice laced with wisdom, "this watch, a relic of our ancestry, carries within it the echoes of our past. But before it becomes yours, venture into the bustling city and seek the jeweler's appraisal. Discover the monetary worth they attach to this timeless artifact."

Filled with anticipation and a touch of skepticism, the son embarked on his journey, the watch carefully cradled within his palm. Returning to his father, the son's voice trembled with disappointment as he shared the outcome. "Father," he uttered, "they offered a mere $200 for this watch, deeming its value solely in its age."

Undeterred by the initial appraisal, the father's eyes sparkled with unwavering belief. "Son," he whispered, "the world holds more secrets than we can fathom. Seek another destination, a place that will see beyond the surface, where the true essence of this treasure can be revealed."

With a newfound resolve, the son ventured to the humble pawnshop, a realm where hidden gems often found their sanctuary. Yet, as he returned to his father's side, a tinge of despondency clung to his words. "Father," he sighed, "the pawnshop could only offer a mere $50, for they saw nothing beyond a superficial scratch that marred its surface."

Undeterred, the father, a beacon of unwavering wisdom, offered his final counsel. "My son," he imparted, "seek the halls of knowledge, where the guardians of history reside. Show them the watch, for they possess a discerning eye that sees the true worth of the rare and remarkable."

Though skepticism nestled in the recesses of his mind, the son embraced his father's wishes and embarked on a pilgrimage to the museum. As he presented the watch to the curator, an air of anticipation hung in the air, mingling with the whispers of the past. Time seemed to hold its breath as the curator's eyes fell upon the aged timepiece.

Upon the son's return, a radiant smile adorned his face, his voice alive with awe. "Father," he exclaimed, "the curator saw the magnificence of this treasure. They recognized its rarity, its unmatched beauty, and offered an astounding $375,000. They yearned to include it in their hallowed collection of precious antiques."

With a tender smile playing upon his lips, the father embraced his son's astonishment and whispered words that carried the weight of a timeless truth. "Son," he said, his voice infused with a gentle wisdom, "what I sought to reveal through this journey was not merely the worth of the watch, but the profound significance it holds in shaping your perception of self."

"In this vast maze of life, it is essential to remember that the right place, the right people, will recognize your inherent value and cherish you accordingly. Do not allow yourself to be ensnared within the confines of a place that fails to see your worth, for it is there that resentment and dissatisfaction may take root."

The notion of self-worth, of recognizing and embracing one's own value, resonated deeply within the audience. The lessons learned from the watch's journey reverberated through their consciousness, illuminating the path that they must tread.

Guru ji concluded, for when one fails to acknowledge their own worth, they inadvertently find themselves accepting a mere fraction of the abundance that awaits them. Be it in relationships, in their chosen profession, or in the web of friendships, those who are unaware of their true value often settle for another's limited perception of their worth.

The seekers listened; their souls held captive by the enchanting narrative. As Guru Ji's words wove intricate patterns in the air, the story breathed life into their thoughts and kindled a flame of understanding within their hearts.

In that sacred moment, the story became a mirror, reflecting the intricate dance between the professional, familial, social, and personal realms. Each dimension shimmered with newfound clarity, illuminated by the timeless wisdom encapsulated within the tale.

❑

3

Self Confidence

Orange Spectrum

"Experience tells you what to do; confidence allows you to do it."

– Stan Smith

The dawn's gentle embrace ushered in a serene ambiance, setting the stage for a transformative journey that lay ahead. As the participants gathered, their eyes sparkled with an unwavering eagerness, their souls yearning for the profound experience that awaited them. In the realm of tranquil stillness, they prepared themselves for the meditation – a harmonious fusion of mind, body, and spirit.

As the sun's gentle rays caressed the room, Guru Ji greeted all, bidding them a harmonious good morning. With an air of anticipation, he announced that today, amidst the vibrant glow of the yellow spectrum, the essence of "Self Confidence" would unravel before their very eyes.

It was an invitation to embark upon a profound journey of self-discovery, one that would shape their perspectives in unimaginable ways.

In the sanctuary of collective wisdom, Guru Ji sought to illuminate a crucial aspect that hindered their pursuit of self-confidence – the insidious presence of "Limiting Beliefs." With his words infused with profound insights, he drew their attention to a timeless metaphor, that of a baby elephant. Born into a world of boundless potential, this majestic creature's destiny seemed boundless. However, a single physical bond tethered its tiny leg to a wooden post, imposing an illusion of confinement upon its nascent spirit.

Guru Ji painted a vivid portrait of the baby elephant's struggle, illustrating the disparity between its inherent strength and the perceived limitations imposed by that seemingly insignificant chain. As the elephant grew in stature, its physical prowess outmatched the meager resistance of that feeble bond. And yet, the mighty beast remained captive to a belief, a belief forged in the crucible of its formative years, that it could not break free.

Just as the elephant possessed the strength to shatter the chains that bound it, they too harbored untapped reservoirs of potential, awaiting release from the shackles of limiting beliefs. It was these deeply ingrained convictions, he asserted, that posed the most formidable obstacles on the arduous path to self-confidence. With unwavering guidance, he illuminated the transformative power that awaited them once they relinquished the weight of limiting beliefs and embraced the boundless expanse of their true capabilities.

As his words resonated through the room, a flicker of newfound determination danced in the eyes of his disciples. They understood that their journey towards self-confidence necessitated a steadfast dismantling of the mental chains that restrained them.

In the realm of endless possibilities, your mentors stand as beacons of guidance, ready to bestow upon you a transformative framework. Through their wise counsel, introspection shall flourish, and the light of awareness shall illuminate your path. As you embark upon this journey, may the fortunes of destiny smile upon you. Good luck, dear travelers!

In the heart of the gathering, Gopal Ji, a paragon of wisdom, awaited the arrival of his team. With hearts brimming with gratitude, they approached him, acknowledging the profound impact his presence had upon their lives. With a gentle smile, Gopal Ji initiated the sacred exchange, urging his team to shed the shackles of their limiting beliefs.

Rahul stepped forward, his voice resolute and earnest, spoke of his professional journey, acknowledging that he harbored no limiting beliefs within that realm. Instead, he found himself gripped by a sense of unwarranted overconfidence, a double-edged sword that threatened to blind him to his own vulnerabilities. Yet, in the quiet recesses of his soul, a different narrative emerged. Rahul confessed his doubts about his entrepreneurial prowess, an inner voice whispering that perhaps he lacked the requisite qualities to thrive in that domain. Furthermore, a disconcerting thought gnawed at his consciousness, suggesting that his capacity for engaging in altruistic endeavors for the betterment of society remained dubious at best. In the midst of this shared experience, Rahul found solace. He realized that the mere act of vocalizing his doubts and uncertainties was an act of liberation.

Natasha, her heart heavy with untold stories, summoned the courage to share her truth. "I have always carried this gnawing sensation that commitment eludes me, that forever is an elusive concept," she admitted, her voice tinged with a hint of remorse. She pondered if this belief had played a role in the dissolution of her marriage, a bittersweet realization that set her soul adrift. She confessed that she had harbored dreams of establishing her boutiques beyond the borders of her beloved India. Yet, a pervasive anxiety had gripped her, shackling her aspirations and preventing her from taking that bold leap. It was a limiting belief, she acknowledged, one that whispered doubts of her ability to manage such ventures with grace and success.

As she spoke, Natasha's mind wandered, weaving through the memories of her upbringing. The question lingered, like an enigmatic specter, haunting her thoughts.

Had her early years catalyzed the formation of these limiting beliefs? In this crucible of revelation, Natasha embarked on a dual journey of self-discovery and self- healing.

In the stillness of the room, Samantha and Simon sat, their minds attuned to the wisdom that unfolded before them. As the mentor's words lingered in the air, they shared a silent understanding, a collective need for introspection and evaluation. With gratitude in their hearts, they addressed their mentor, their voices filled with earnestness. "Mentor," they spoke in unison, "we need time to reflect on this, to delve deep into the recesses of our souls."

"I wholeheartedly agree," Gopal Ji responded, his voice suffused with warmth. "This journey of self-discovery requires time, the sacred moments of solitude where one can nurture the seeds of introspection." He encouraged each individual to embark upon their personal voyage of reflection, and reunite post lunch.

In the aftermath of their post lunch reunion, Gopal Ji, the harbinger of wisdom, stepped forward to offer his profound insights. "Beliefs," Gopal Ji began, his voice resonating with a depth that stirred the soul, "are the bedrock upon which our perception of reality is built. They take root in the fertile soil of our early years, nourished by the society and culture that shape our upbringing."

As the years unfold, Gopal Ji continued, experience acts as both a crucible and a catalyst, determining the strength or fragility of these beliefs. Life, in its intricate dance, presents us with trials and triumphs, moments of joy and moments of despair. It is through these experiences that the foundations of our beliefs are tested, either fortified or shaken to their very core.

In this sacred space of introspection, Gopal Ji imparted a revelation of profound significance. Knowledge, he proclaimed, was a potent instrument, a key that unlocked the door to self-discovery. It bestowed upon us the ability to scrutinize and evaluate the beliefs that shaped our perceptions, offering a lens through which we could examine the very fabric of our existence.

Knowledge, like a guiding light in the darkness, illuminated the depths of our consciousness. It endowed us with the power to question, to challenge the dogmas that once held us captive. Armed with this formidable tool, we could embark upon a journey of self- reflection, peering through the veils of societal conditioning to uncover our own truth.

Samantha's voice, filled with longing, pierced the air as she posed her heartfelt question. "Mentor," she implored, her eyes shimmering with a glimmer of hope, "what can we do to cultivate and nurture our self-confidence?" A gentle smile curved upon the mentor's lips as he acknowledged the beauty of Samantha's inquiry. "Ah, my dear," he responded, his voice a soothing balm for the soul, "you have ventured into a realm of profound self-discovery.

There are myriad pathways that lead to the strengthening of one's self-confidence."

He began to unveil the secrets, like precious pearls strung together on a delicate thread. "Firstly," he revealed, "it is crucial to remind yourself of your own achievements, both great and small.

Each triumph, no matter how seemingly insignificant, contributes to building of your confidence." The mentor continued, bestowing upon them the gift of wisdom. "Remember," he whispered, his voice carrying the weight of truth, "every individual is a radiant flame, shining with a brilliance all their own. Do not fall victim to the toxic trap of comparison. Embrace your uniqueness, for it is the very essence that sets you apart, illuminating your path towards self- assurance."

But the mentor's revelations did not end there. He delved deeper, reaching into the recesses of their hearts. "Lastly," he imparted, "release the weight of guilt that burdens your spirit. We are all flawed beings, bound to make mistakes along this intricate fabric of life.

Do not allow guilt to define you or hold you captive. Let go of the shackles of remorse and pave the way for self-confidence to flourish."

As his words washed over them, Samantha and her companions felt a sense of liberation. The mentor had gifted them with a roadmap to self-confidence, a guiding light in the vast expanse of their own self-discovery. They understood that by nurturing their accomplishments, embracing their individuality, and shedding the heavy cloak of guilt, they could embark upon a transformative journey towards unshakable self-assurance.

Simon, with a hint of trepidation dancing in his eyes, mustered the courage to seek a much-needed clarification. His voice, laced with vulnerability, trembled as he shared his innermost desire. "Mentor," he began, his words hanging in the air, "within the realm of my insurance portfolio, I have nurtured a robust client base. However, a longing persists within me to delve into the world of property dealing. Yet, I find myself shackled by a lack of self-confidence. Could you, in your boundless wisdom, offer me some guidance, some tangible suggestions to overcome this hurdle?"

Gopal Ji, the sage of wisdom, broke the silence that enveloped the room, "My dear Simon," he began, his voice imbued with a gentle yet resolute tone, "let us not forget the golden rule, the trinity of the 3 P's: Passion, Practice, and Patience."

"Passion," he emphasized, "I can see the flickering flame of fervor within you. Nurture it, for passion is the driving force that propels us forward. Cultivate an insatiable thirst for knowledge in the realm of property dealing. Immerse yourself in its intricacies, devour books, attend workshops, and seek the guidance of seasoned mentors."

"Practice," he declared, his voice tinged with unwavering determination, "is the crucible in which dreams are forged into reality. Develop your skills and refine your understanding of the subject. Dedicate yourself to honing the art of presentation, understanding the unique needs and inconveniences of your clients, and offering them solutions that not only address their concerns but exceed their expectations."

"Patience," he revealed, his voice tinged with the wisdom of the ages, "is the virtue that breathes life into our aspirations. Understand that greatness is not achieved in a day, nor is it handed to us on a silver platter. Embrace the journey, knowing that each step, no matter how small, brings you closer to your goals. Be steadfast in your efforts, and trust that the universe shall conspire to support you on your path."

As Gopal Ji's words settled within their hearts, Simon and his companions felt a renewed sense of purpose. They understood that the road ahead would be arduous, but armed with the trinity of the 3 P's, they were ready to embrace the challenges that lay before them. The group disbursed for a short break to take part in the mediation followed by Guru Ji's conclusion.

As the team assembled in the grand hall, Guru Ji's presence cast a radiant glow upon the gathering. "My dear friends," Guru Ji began, their voice resonating with a profound sense of contentment, "today fills my heart with an abundance of joy. Throughout the day, I witnessed each one of you carve out precious moments, immersing yourselves in the sanctuary of introspection. I applaud you, for in giving yourself the gift of undivided attention, you have embarked upon a journey of self-discovery that is worthy of celebration."

"Let us not diminish the significance of what we have learned today," Guru Ji began, their words cascading like melodic notes of a symphony. "For within the realm of self-confidence, there are two essential ingredients that serve as beacons on the path to self- confidence —Awareness and Clarity of Purpose."

"In this grand curtain of life," Guru Ji continued, his voice infused with a deep sense of reverence, "Clarity of Purpose becomes the guiding light that illuminates our journey. When we possess a clear vision, when we embrace a purpose that resonates with the very core of our being, the universe aligns itself to aid us in our pursuit. It is through this alignment that the fragments of our being come together, and the elements of mindset, self-motivation, and beliefs seamlessly harmonize, creating a symphony of inner strength and unwavering self-confidence."

"Ah, but let us not forget the enchanting dance of Awareness," Guru Ji whispered, his voice like a gentle breeze caressing their souls. "It is through the awakening of our senses, the expansion of our horizons, that we traverse the landscapes of knowledge. By immersing ourselves in the subject that fuels our passions, by seeking wisdom from mentors, coaches and guides, we unlock the door to awareness. And within this sacred chamber, we find the seeds of self-discovery, germinating and blossoming into a dosser of understanding that nurtures our self-confidence."

And so, armed with the twin pillars of Awareness and Clarity of Purpose, the participants embarked upon a journey of self-realization. They knew that this path would not be without challenges, but they embraced each obstacle as an opportunity for growth. With every step, their self-confidence swelled, their spirits soared, and the symphony of their inner strength resounded through the chambers of their souls.

❑

4

Empathy

Green Spectrum

"Kindness should become the natural way of life, not the exception"

- Buddha

As the sun's gentle rays pierced through the gray canopy, a delicate drizzle embraced the morning, the gentle patter of raindrops harmonized with the rustle of leaves, creating a soothing melody that seemed to speak to the depths of the seeker's being. Seekers of inner peace ventured forth, seeking solace within the embrace of meditation.

Guru Ji, extended a warm welcome to the gathering that had assembled in anticipation. With an air of profound wisdom, he announced, "Ladies and gentlemen, today I shall introduce you to the most exquisite facet of our being—the essence that resides within each and every one of us: the Heart." Green spectrum which can be summed up as "Empathy" is something which we all will dwell upon today.

"In a world fraught with complexities and personal battles," Guru Ji continued, his voice resonating with earnestness, "empathy emerges as a beacon of light, illuminating the path towards harmony and genuine human connection. It is an art—an art that allows us to step into another's shoes, to comprehend their joys and sorrows from their very frame of existence."

"Dear friends," he emphasized, his gaze sweeping across the attentive crowd, "empathy is the cornerstone upon which healthy relationships and love are built. It is the nurturing soil that cultivates kindness and respect, allowing them to bloom in the garden of our souls."

In the web of humanity, nestled within the heart of every individual, lies a precious seed—the seed of empathy. It is a gift bestowed upon us, varying in its readiness to blossom, influenced by the intricate design of karmic patterns. Some are fortunate, naturally blessed with the ingredients for this seed to flourish, while others embark upon a journey of self-discovery to cultivate and nurture its growth. As we gather here, united by the profound threads of our shared humanity, it is vital to recognize our inherent kinship. We are not merely strangers passing through the ebb and flow of time. No, dear friends, we are divine brothers and sisters, interconnected in ways that transcend the confines of this temporal existence.

Embrace the path of empathy, dear seekers, for it is the golden key that unlocks the gates to understanding and compassion. Let us foster this divine seed within ourselves and in one another, nurturing its growth with every interaction, every word, and every gesture.

Together, as we embark on this collective transformation, we shall witness the emergence of a world where empathy binds us in a tapestry of unity, love, and interconnectedness.

Guru Ji concluded his discourse, his eyes filled with a gleam of hope for the future. “Let empathy guide our interactions, let it infuse our words and actions with compassion,” he said. The applause that followed resonated with newfound inspiration, as each person present pledged to nurture the seed of empathy within their hearts.

Amidst this air of curiosity and excitement, they encountered Gopal Ji, a figure of wisdom and grace. With a humble gesture of folded hands, he extended a warm welcome, his eyes reflecting a deep wellspring of knowledge. “Welcome,” Gopal Ji began, his voice gentle yet commanding, “to the luminous realm of the green light— the gateway that shall illuminate the path toward the realms that lie beyond. But, let us pause for a moment, and in a lighter vein, view life through the prism of a traffic light."

As smiles flickered across their faces, Gopal Ji playfully intertwined a mundane symbol with profound insights. "In this journey called life, many find themselves ensnared by the hues of red, orange, or yellow lights," Gopal Ji continued, his voice tinged with a wisdom earned through experience. "Impatience overtakes us as we yearn for progress, for the green light that beckons us forward. Yet, it is in these moments of waiting, of exercising patience, that the magic of life unfolds."

"Notice," Gopal Ji pointed out with a knowing smile, "that these lights continue to manifest as we keep traveling, ceaselessly moving forward. Such is the essence of life—a perpetual dance along the intricate network of spectrums. It is the art of striking a balance, of embracing each spectrum with grace and resilience."

A shared chuckle filled the air as Gopal Ji acknowledged his philosophical musings. "Ah, it seems I have stumbled upon the realms of introspection," he admitted, his laughter echoing through the space. "But let us not dwell upon my ramblings. Instead, let us turn our ears to the voices of each member present."

Rahul took a bold step forward, his heart brimming with an inexplicable joy. For Rahul, a person driven by a relentless pursuit of self-improvement, today's revelations held the key to nourishing the seed of empathy that resided within him. With unflinching honesty, Rahul acknowledged the profound impact this gathering had already had on his journey of self-discovery. It was a revelation that struck him to his very core. Never before had he truly listened, sincerely absorbed the words of others without the burden of his own preconceived notions. It was a revelation that unveiled a newfound appreciation for the unique perspectives and experiences shared by his fellow team members. With a humble smile, Rahul looked ahead, eager to partake in the beauty that lay in the collective wisdom of his team members, ready to continue his quest for empathy and understanding.

Gratitude filled Samantha's heart as she expressed her appreciation to the mentor who had guided them with unwavering support. With a voice laced with sincerity, she acknowledged the mentor's remarkable display of empathy—attentive listening and gentle guidance that had touched the depths of their souls. Yet, Samantha recognized that the journey had only just begun. The sprout of empathy, though promising, required nourishment and care to flourish into a magnificent blossoming flower. With unwavering resolve, Samantha vowed to cultivate her inner garden, to tend to the soil of her being with patience and self-reflection. She knew that unlocking the full potential of her empathetic nature required inner work—an exploration of her own beliefs, biases, and limitations.

Within the depths of his being, Simon felt a profound sense of gratitude for the presence of his beloved partner. In her, he discovered a harmonious balance, a perfect embodiment of empathy. As Simon reflected upon his journey, he couldn't help but acknowledge the observations made by those who knew him well.

It was a poignant realization that when others spoke his name, they seldom associated him with sadness, frustration, or anger. Even during those weeks when his conversations yielded no tangible results, it was his wife who illuminated his path with a wisdom that nourished the seed of empathy within him. "Simon," she had gently spoken, her words a balm to his wounded spirit, "I understand your desire to sell the policy, but perhaps the client lacked the financial means to commit. Instead of doubting your own abilities or becoming upset with the client, let us offer a prayer for their prosperity."

Natasha extended her appreciation to her father, whose words of wisdom had become the guiding light of her entrepreneurial journey. she vividly recalled her father's profound insight—a simple yet profound truth—that when one sells perfumes, a hint of its fragrance lingers on their own hands. This realization became the bedrock of their business's core value—a philosophy that Natasha passionately referred to as "Sharing Dreams." It was a philosophy that transcended mere transactions, for Natasha and her team aimed to weave dreams into the very fabric of their interactions. With a sense of pride, she revealed that their boutique catered to a diverse range of budgets, ensuring that the dreams of each and every client were treated with utmost importance.

Natasha's voice resonated with conviction as she revealed a deeper understanding—one that had crystallized through her own journey of empathy and connection. She had come to realize that empathy was the vital thread that wove together the web of relationships, love, and trust. It was the cornerstone upon which their boutique thrived, for it allowed them to truly understand and embrace the dreams of their clients. But Natasha's vision extended far beyond the confines of her boutique. She recognized that empathy had the power to fuel not only personal connections but also the growth and prosperity of their business. It was a belief that fueled her confidence in the team she had assembled—a team that understood the delicate art of empathy and its transformative potential.

With a gracious smile adorning his face, Gopal Ji extended his heartfelt appreciation to the gathered audience. He exuded an air of wisdom, ready to unveil a secret known to few—the existence of three distinct realms of empathy.

The first realm he unraveled was known as affective empathy—a remarkable ability to delve into the depth of another's emotions, to comprehend their innermost turmoil, and to respond with unfathomable understanding. It was a skill that transcended the ordinary, allowing one to navigate the intricate nuances of human sentiment, offering solace and compassion in times of joy or sorrow.

Gopal Ji then delved into the realm of somatic empathy—a mysterious connection that transcended the boundaries of the mind and transcended into the realm of the physical. Here, one could feel another's experiences as though they were their own, experiencing the ebb and flow of sensations coursing through their veins.

Finally, he unveiled the profound realm of cognitive empathy—a realm where one could traverse the landscapes of another's mind, uncovering the intricacies of their thoughts, fears, and desires. It was a realm that required profound insight and an unwavering ability to perceive beyond the surface, to understand the complexities of another's mental state.

The time had come to momentarily part ways and nourish their bodies, for soon they would embark upon a journey fraught with challenges—the exploration of empathy's barriers.

With eager anticipation twinkling in their eyes, the team turned their attention to Gopal Ji, their revered mentor. Gopal Ji asked "what you think could be the barriers to empathy, any views?" Team looked at each other and asked their mentor to enlighten them with the barriers.

Gopal Ji proclaimed, his voice carrying the weight of undeniable truth. “Within the depths of our minds, cognitive biases lay in wait, wielding their invisible influence upon our perceptions. They possess the power to distort our very gaze upon the world, shaping reality to their whims.” “And so,” Gopal Ji continued, his eyes brimming with sagacity, “we find ourselves confined within the narrow corridors of our own perspectives, unable to fathom the vastness that lies beyond. The very essence of empathy eludes us, for these biases, like an impenetrable fog, hinder our ability to comprehend the world through another’s eyes.”

In the realm of human connection, a shadow lingers—a dark abyss known as dehumanization. The maestro of words, with his literary brush poised, weaves a tale that exposes the fragile threads of empathy. “Let us delve into the treacherous depths of dehumanization, where the seeds of indifference take root.

Enveloped in the cloak of ignorance, we often find solace in the false belief that those who differ from us are somehow fundamentally disconnected from our own human experience.”

In the realm of human judgment, a nefarious specter lurks—the haunting shadows of victim blaming. “And so, dear friends, let us explore the treacherous terrain of victim blaming, where the threads of empathy are often frayed. In the face of unspeakable suffering, many succumb to the temptation of assigning blame to the very souls who have been wounded. It is a delicate dance upon the precipice of ignorance."

In the hallowed sanctuary of the meditation hall, seekers of truth gathered, their souls entwined in a quest for enlightenment. Guru Ji began, his voice resonating with a profound truth. "Recognition, my friends, is the first step on the path of transformation. We must acknowledge the presence of biases within us, for it is only through acceptance that we can embark on the journey of overcoming them." Silence enveloped the room as the seekers absorbed his words, their hearts fluttering with a newfound understanding. To recognize one's biases, to confront the shadows that cloud our perception—this was the gateway to find balance in this spectrum.

Guru Ji continued, his voice like a gentle breeze stirring the depths of their souls. "In the realm of compassion, we can make a difference. By practicing empathy, by standing tall in solidarity with others, we begin to dismantle the walls that divide." A chorus of nodding heads followed Guru Ji's words, as the seekers embraced the power that lay within their grasp.

"Expand your horizons, my dear ones," Guru Ji urged, his eyes shimmering with unwavering resolve. "Seek knowledge, for it is through understanding that our biases crumble. Embrace the vastness of the world, for it is within its rich diversity that empathy flourishes."

"And let us not forget, my dear seekers, the future lies in the hands of our children," Guru Ji proclaimed, his voice now soft as a lullaby. "In raising empathetic souls, we sow the seeds of a more compassionate world. Teach them the beauty of empathy, and watch as they carry the torch of compassion forward."

❑

5

Self-Expression

Blue Spectrum

"Live life as though nobody is watching, and express yourself as though everyone is listening"

- Nelson Mandela

The sun-kissed chamber of meditation buzzed with anticipation, for today's session held a hint of intrigue. The atmosphere crackled with curiosity as the meditators settled into their sacred spaces, their eyes drawn to the flickering flame of a single candle that danced before them. Guru Ji began, his words floating upon the air like whispers of enchantment. "Today, we shall embark on a unique path, a dance with the flame that shall kindle the depths of our focus."

As the session drew to a close, a palpable serenity washed over the room, painting smiles upon the faces of the meditators. They felt a newfound sense of clarity, a harmonious symphony of thoughts dancing in their minds. The flame had wielded its magic, bestowing upon them the gift of heightened focus.

Guru Ji's voice, resonating with the essence of the blue sky above. "Welcome, dear seekers, to the realm of self-expression," he greeted, his eyes twinkling with a knowing light. "Today, we bask in the hues of the blue spectrum, for it is within this vast expanse that our soul finds its wings."

"Dear souls," he began, his words carrying the weight of revelation, "let us delve into the profound truth that our expression knows no bounds. It extends far beyond the mere confines of language, permeating every aspect of our existence. Our eyes, our faces, the very fabric that adorns our bodies—all bear witness to the essence of our expression."

Silence settled upon the room, as the seekers pondered the magnitude of this revelation. They realized that even in the absence of words, in the hush of silence, they were still communicating. Their very presence spoke volumes, conveying the depths of their emotions and the stories etched upon their souls.

"In this grand spectrum of expression," the sage continued, his voice resonating with wisdom, "lies the key to our understanding. What are we expressing? Why do we share our thoughts and emotions with the world? And how do we choose to reveal our innermost selves? These questions guide us on a sacred path of self- discovery."

Dear friends, I invite you to embark on a profound journey," the sage urged, his voice a beacon of guidance. "Uncover the layers of your being, explore the depths of your true expression. Seek the answers to these questions, for in doing so, you enrich not only your own journey but also the lives of those you encounter." A chorus of anticipation filled the air, as the seekers embraced the quest that lay before them. They knew that their mentors would serve as guiding lights, illuminating the path to self-discovery.

In the realm of Gopal Ji's domain, his team eagerly gathered, their hearts brimming with anticipation. What secrets would their revered mentor unveil today? Thoughts swirled through their minds, dancing with curiosity. Yet, to their astonishment, Gopal Ji, the harbinger of wisdom, chose a different path. "Dear friends," he began, his voice a gentle breeze of reassurance, "let me ease your minds and offer insights to the questions that have stirred within you. Today, I shall begin by unraveling the very essence of our expression."

With a knowing smile, Gopal Ji commenced his exposition, his words weaving a cobweb of understanding. "When we delve into the realms of what are we expressing, my dear friends, we uncover a vast array of treasures. Thoughts, feelings, opinions, and emotions–these are the elements with which we paint our inner world upon the canvas of existence."

In the realm of insightful inquiry, Rahul, with a spark of curiosity, raised his hand, his eyes shining with a hunger for knowledge. "Gopal Ji," he ventured, "isn't it true that our beliefs form an integral part of our expression?" Gopal Ji, the master of enlightenment, bestowed upon Rahul a nod of appreciation. "Ah, Rahul," he acknowledged, "what a profound question you pose. Let us, then, embark on the journey of unraveling the how do we express."

"Dear seekers," Gopal Ji began, his voice a symphony of clarity, "within the realms of expression, our belief systems, values, and attitude intertwine, align. These dimensions, like gentle guides, shape the very mechanism through which we express ourselves." As his words unfurled, the seekers absorbed the profound truth that resonated within their souls. They recognized that their expression flowed from the deep wellsprings of their core beliefs, the guiding stars that illuminated their path.

Within the realm of eager inquiry, Samantha, her voice tinged with a hint of uncertainty, summoned the courage to speak. "Gopal Ji," she began hesitantly, "forgive me if my question seems naive. I yearn to understand, is there truly no such thing as a dumb question?" Gopal Ji, the paragon of wisdom, his eyes brimming with compassion, reassured Samantha. "Fear not, dear Samantha," he replied, his voice a soothing balm. "In this sacred space of knowledge-seeking, every question, no matter how it may seem, holds significance and holds the potential for growth."

With newfound confidence, Samantha unveiled the next layer of her inquiry. "Gopal Ji," she ventured, her voice laced with vulnerability, "there are moments when I find myself hesitant to express my true self. Is it truly important to express, and if so, how can I navigate this journey of self-expression?"

Gopal Ji, the harbinger of guidance, acknowledged Samantha's yearning with a gentle nod. "Dear Samantha," he empathized, "your question resonates deeply within the hearts of many. Let me offer you my guiding light, as we explore the importance of why we need to express."

"Dear friends," he began, his voice filled with gentle urgency, "by locking away the depths of your emotions, you risk a catastrophic explosion, an eruption born from the turbulent storms within.

For within the confines of a bottled heart, the pressure of unexpressed feelings mounts, seeking release in the most unexpected of ways."

Gopal Ji, the guardian of revelation, continued to unveil the intricate design of human connection. "And yet, dear seekers," he declared, his voice tinged with empathy, "there is yet another consequence to this self-imposed silence. By withholding the truth of who you are, you deny others the opportunity to truly know you. In the absence of your authentic expression, they are left to piece together fragmented impressions, shaping their perception of you through their limited perspectives."

Gopal Ji, the harbinger of clarity, gently unveiled yet another layer of truth. "Dear Samantha," he proclaimed, his voice carrying the weight of compassion, "the suppression of emotions, the regression of your innermost feelings, holds within it the potential for increased stress and anxiety. For when the soul's voice is stifled, the spirit suffers, burdened by the weight of unexpressed truths." He concluded "expression is the gateway through which we share the essence of our being with the world. It is the thread that weaves the fabric of connection and understanding, fostering authentic relationships and allowing our true selves to blossom."

Within the hallowed halls of wisdom, Simon's voice pierced the air, carrying with it a longing for understanding. "Gopal Ji," he inquired, his voice laced with curiosity, "what are the shackles that constrict our ability to express?"

Gopal Ji, the master of enlightenment, his eyes shimmering with appreciation, embraced the question with open arms. "Ah, Simon," he exclaimed, "a truly remarkable query. Let us, dear seekers, indulge in the nourishment of sustenance before we embark upon this enlightening discussion."

In the realm of self-expression, mentor enlightened his team to the myriad obstacles that can impede path of self-expression. Allow me, dear companions, to divulge the two principal aspects that lie at the heart of this conundrum. The first, a formidable adversary known as the "Fear of Conflict," is a frequent assailant that shackles our tongues and binds our emotions. Far too often, we find ourselves reticent and unwilling to reveal our true sentiments, lest they inflict harm upon another's delicate soul. And so, we suppress our innermost thoughts, only to ruefully lament later, tormented by the unspoken words and unfulfilled desires that linger within us. Alas, the regret that follows serves as a painful reminder of the opportunities missed and the profound longing to have courageously expressed our heartfelt truth.

Within the coil of self-expression, our journey continues as we confront yet another formidable impediment—the enigma known as "What People Will Think?" Ah, dear seekers, it is a tangled web indeed, for it is not the people themselves who occupy their precious thoughts with our every word and deed; nay, it is our own minds that concoct this illusion. This concern, born of our own insecurities and fears, weaves a suffocating cloak around our authentic selves, rendering us captives to the opinions of others. The incessant questions plague our hearts and minds: How will they perceive us? Will our actions meet with their approval or disdain? Alas, dear friends, we must not allow these inquiries to dictate the course of our self-expression. We must not surrender the reins of our true essence to the whims of external expectations. For if we begin to tailor our words, actions, and very beings to conform to the expectations of others, we shall forever be bound, unable to unfurl the beautiful tapestry of our genuine selves upon the world's stage.

Natasha's voice resounded with gratitude as she extended her heartfelt thanks to the mentor, her eyes shimmering with newfound enlightenment. "Oh, esteemed mentor," she spoke, her words dripping with reverence, "your wisdom has illuminated our minds, guiding us through the complexities of introspection as we grappled with those three profound questions posed earlier today." Her curiosity piqued, she ventured further, her voice trembling with anticipation. "I wonder, dear mentor, if you could bestow upon us your divine knowledge regarding the activities that might serve as catalysts for our journey towards self-expression?"

A gentle smile adorned the face of Gopal Ji, a twinkle of admiration glimmering within his eyes. "Ah, my dear Natasha," he replied, his voice saturated with warmth and appreciation, "truly, your hunger for personal growth and unwavering thirst for knowledge are commendable. You seek to enhance your being, to unfurl the petals of your inner bloom. Fear not, for I shall unveil before you an array of remarkable activities that shall pave the way to self-expression, illuminating your path like stars in the night sky."

As we continue our enchanting odyssey towards the realm of self-expression, I shall impart upon you, dear seekers, an exquisite suggestion—a key that unlocks the vault of your deepest emotions and experiences. Behold, the mighty power of the Writing! where ink dances upon parchment, where poetry, prose, blogging, journaling, and the art of creative writing intertwine to form a collage of self- expression. Within these sacred realms, the intangible essence of your being finds solace, transforming into something tangible and real, bared to the world in all its raw beauty. Embracing the practice of writing, nearly every day, shall be your guiding compass, leading you towards a path of fulfillment and authenticity. For in the act of writing, you are compelled to search for the precise words and expressions that shall best convey your message to the eager hearts.

The wondrous alchemy of creative expression—a transformative elixir for your weary soul, a catalyst that ignites the flames of emotional healing. When your art becomes a conduit for self- expression, a vessel through which the depths of your being pour forth, its value transcends mere aesthetics. Immerse yourself, dear souls, in the sacred act of creative self-expression. Observe as the ethereal tendrils of your mental imagery take shape, manifesting before you in physical form. Through strokes of a paintbrush or pen, through the grace of dance or the melody of song, your feelings, emotions, and thoughts shall find their tangible reflection. Let your voice soar through song, your body move with grace in dance, or channel your creativity through the art of collaging, coloring, composing music, or even crafting.

As the day drew to a close, the seekers converged in the hallowed hall, their hearts brimming with anticipation for Guru Ji's final discourse. A gentle smile graced the lips of the revered Guru as he extended his warm welcome to all who had gathered. "Today," he began, his voice resonating with wisdom accumulated through countless journeys of self-expression, "you have delved into the depths of self-expression, unraveling its multi dimensions." His words hung in the air, like delicate tendrils of insight weaving a fabric of understanding.

Yet, dear seekers, there is one facet that beckons our attention—a concept that I have come to term as 'Conditioned Self Expression.' Guru Ji's gaze swept across the room, his eyes sparkling with empathy, as he unraveled the truth that lay hidden within this enigmatic phrase. He unveiled the masks that this conditioned self- expression may don—the visage of control, the facade of aggression, the rebellion that simmers beneath the surface, or even the jester's mirth, striving to elicit laughter and belong amidst the psychological tension of denying one's authentic self.

Let it be known, dear souls, that I do not dismiss the need for guidance, boundaries, or emotional regulation in our children. However, I implore you to lend an ear to their self-expression, to validate their innermost desires and fears, so they may feel truly heard and understood. By offering explanations, enlightening them on how their behavior impacts both themselves and others, we equip them with vital information, empowering them to make informed choices as they journey forward.

Within the intricacies of self-expression, a profound truth reveals itself—our thoughts, emotions, and very essence are intertwined with the depths of our inner being. As I stand before you, dear friends, I wholeheartedly beseech you to embrace the transformative power of self-acceptance—a gateway to authentic self-expression.

Imagine, if you will, a world where you wholeheartedly accept yourself, embracing every fiber of your being with open arms. It may seem a simple task, but rest assured, dear seekers, the journey to self- acceptance is not without its challenges. From the earliest days of our existence, we are molded by external forces, taught what to say, what to conceal, how to behave, and how to present ourselves to the world. Yet, amidst this intricately woven fabric of societal expectations, lies the urgent need to reconnect with our true selves.

Turn your gaze inward, dear voyagers, and embark upon the profound quest to discover the essence of your being. Listen intently to the whispers of your soul, for they hold the keys to unlocking your authentic self. Grant yourself permission to acknowledge the kaleidoscope of emotions that reside within you, and honor the sacredness of your own feelings. It is through this journey of self- awareness and self-acceptance that the gates of self-expression shall swing open wide, ushering forth a torrent of unrestrained authentic self-expression. Let your voice resound with the harmonious symphony of your being, as the world beholds the exquisite masterpiece that is uniquely and undeniably YOU.

❑

6

Self-Knowledge

Indigo Spectrum

"The essence of knowledge is Self-Knowledge"

– Plato

In the sacred haven of the meditation hall, seekers congregated, their spirits aflame with anticipation. Guru Ji, the guiding light amidst their journey of self-discovery, beckoned them to a new focal point—the space between the eyebrows, just above the bridge of the nose. Eager to absorb the wisdom bestowed upon them, the attendees obediently directed their gaze as instructed. Yet, as the session unfolded, a subtle heaviness began to settle upon their minds, casting a shadow of unease upon the tranquil atmosphere. Whispers of discomfort rustled through the hall, as the weight upon their heads grew more palpable.

Within the sacred sanctuary of the gathering, Guru Ji's soothing voice resonated, acknowledging the discomfort that had nestled within the hearts of some seekers. "Fear not, dear seekers," he reassured, his words a balm to their troubled spirits. "Relax, for the weight that rests upon your heads shall soon dissipate, leaving only tranquility in its wake."

Eyes filled with curiosity and anticipation turned towards Guru Ji, their gazes fixed upon the wise sage. Today, he revealed, they would embark upon a profound exploration of the indigo spectrum—an ethereal realm intricately intertwined with the profound concept of self-knowledge.

With gentle grace, Guru Ji beckoned the seekers to view this spectrum through two distinct lenses—both transactional and spiritual. Seeking to demystify this intricate concept, he painted a vivid analogy upon the canvas of their minds. "Imagine, if you will, the vast realm of sports," Guru Ji continued, his words dancing upon the air like delicate brushstrokes. "In this realm, we encounter two roles—the players and the spectators. Our mentors, will serve as the guiding lights, leading you all on a transformative journey of self-discovery, unveiling the depths of our being through both transactional and spiritual lenses."

Transactional, he explained, captured the essence of the player— the active participant in life's grand game. It was a realm where one could delve into the intricate dynamics of action and consequence. Yet, dear seekers, there existed another facet—the realm of the spectator, resonating with the very essence of spirituality. In this sacred space, one observed the grand dance of existence, embracing the profound wisdom that arises from quiet contemplation and detached observation.

As the team gathered, anticipation hung in the air like an invisible veil. Gopal Ji, their trusted guide, awaited their arrival, his presence emanating a sense of calm and wisdom. Eager to share their thoughts, the team voiced their concerns—the session had left them with lingering confusion, an uncertainty that needed to be unraveled.

Gopal Ji nodded, acknowledging their yearning for clarity. "Fear not, my dear friends," he reassured, his voice gentle yet resolute. "Today, let us embark on a journey of understanding together. I invite any one of you to step forward and share your thoughts."

Simon, his curiosity burning bright, stepped into the spotlight. "I have a question," he began, his voice filled with eagerness. "I've come to realize that I am both the spectator and the player. But how can this be? I hope my question doesn't come across as impolite."

Gopal Ji smiled warmly, his eyes brimming with compassion. "Not at all, dear Simon," he reassured. "Your observation is valid, and it holds the key to unraveling the mystery that lies before us. Allow me to guide you through a series of memories, and perhaps, the truth shall reveal itself."

Pausing for a moment, Gopal Ji encouraged Simon to delve into his memories, to recall a beautiful moment from his school days.

After a thoughtful pause, Simon's face lit up with a reminiscent glow. "I remember receiving a trophy for winning a debate competition," he shared, a hint of pride evident in his voice.

Gopal Ji's eyes twinkled with delight. "That's wonderful!" he exclaimed. "Now, dear Simon, reflect upon a memory from your college days." Without hesitation, Simon's words spilled forth, brimming with joy. "In my final year, I mustered the courage to propose to the woman I loved, and she agreed. It remains one of the fondest memories from that time."

Gopal Ji nodded; his voice filled with gentle wisdom. "You see, dear Simon, you are the player in the realms of debate, love, and even insurance. But simultaneously, you also embody the essence of the spectator, observing the journey of your own life unfold before you. In this duality lies a profound truth—a truth that resonates with each and every one of us."

The team, their eyes wide with newfound understanding, absorbed the profoundness of Gopal Ji's words. Their guide continued, his voice a soothing melody. "Dear friends, Simon's journey mirrors our own. We are all players and spectators, intertwined in the intricate dance of life.

Embrace this truth, for within it lies the key to unlocking a deeper understanding of our own existence."

In the midst of the gathering, Rahul's voice rose with a burning curiosity, his words punctuating the air. "As the player in this grand game of life, I believe that enhancing my self-knowledge would undoubtedly influence the outcome of the game. Am I on the right path with this thinking?" Gopal Ji, with a serene smile, nodded in affirmation. "Indeed, dear Rahul, your understanding is astute," he replied, his voice carrying a touch of wisdom.

"For you see, self-knowledge is the gateway to self-mastery—a journey of profound transformation. By delving deep into the realms of self-awareness and embracing honest self-assessments, we gain invaluable insights that empower us to make positive changes and master various aspects of our lives." "In this voyage of self-discovery, self-knowledge grants us the ability to craft a meaningful narrative—a fabric that weaves together the threads of our past, present, and future. It offers us a sense of continuity over time, allowing us to understand the interconnectedness of our experiences.

For, you see, self-knowledge is the catalyst that propels us towards ambitious pursuits, be it in the realm of projects, relationships, or the myriad challenges that await us. It is a beacon that guides us towards the vast horizons of our potential, urging us to transcend the boundaries of what we once believed possible.

With a heart brimming with gratitude, Natasha turned to the Mentor, her eyes alight with newfound understanding. "I truly comprehend the significance of self-knowledge now," she expressed, her voice filled with sincerity. "But I wonder, why haven't I prioritized it in my everyday life?"

Gopal Ji, ever the sage, smiled warmly at Natasha's inquiry. "My dear, you've stumbled upon a profound realization," he replied, his words dripping with wisdom. "To shed light on this, let me share a thought: Just as when we're driving, we must be aware of our blind spots, the areas we cannot naturally see. To mitigate this, side mirrors are cleverly positioned at a 90-degree angle, ensuring that we have a clear view and preventing any untoward accidents."

He paused for a moment, allowing the metaphor to settle within Natasha's mind. Then, in a hushed tone, he continued, "In the grand theater of life, these blind spots manifest as unconscious processes. They slyly distort our access to self-knowledge, hindering us from truly understanding ourselves. These biases silently influence the formation of our self-perception, clouding our judgment and obstructing our path to self-knowledge."

The Mentor's voice resonated through the room, captivating the audience with every word. "Ah, my dear seekers," the Mentor continued, "let us now delve into the treacherous realm of self-deception. It is a cunning phenomenon, a deceptive dance of wishful thinking that we engage in, often unaware of its seductive allure. In this state, we cling to beliefs that align with our desires, regardless of their lack of solid foundation. We craft a narrative that suits our whims, weaving a cobweb of illusions that shield us from the harsh realities of truth."

The Mentor's voice carried a note of caution as they continued, "To guard against this treacherous trap, dear seekers, we must arm ourselves with the weapon of factual information. We must seek a deep understanding of our emotional landscape, our unique personality traits, the intricate web of our relationships, the patterns that govern our behaviors, the very core of our opinions, beliefs, values, needs, goals, preferences, and the fabric of our social identity."

Samantha, her eyes sparkling with a profound sense of self- awareness. "Gopal Ji," she began, her voice filled with curiosity, "I have embarked on a journey of self-discovery, learning the delicate art of balance. With this newfound understanding, can I consider it as self-knowledge in the game of life I am currently playing?"

Gopal Ji's eyes gleamed with admiration, acknowledging Samantha's astute observation. "Dear Samantha," he responded, a gentle smile gracing his lips, "you have raised a pertinent point indeed. Your awareness of your presence and purpose is undeniably a crucial aspect of self-knowledge. It is the first step towards unraveling the mysteries of your being."

The room hung in anticipation as Gopal Ji continued, his words carrying the weight of wisdom. "However, Samantha, self-knowledge encompasses more than just self-awareness. It beckons you to dive deeper within yourself, to explore the intricate nuances of your mind and soul. Introspection becomes the key, as you navigate the complex ways of your thoughts and emotions."

He paused, allowing his words to settle within Samantha's mind. "You must ask yourself, is your mind open to new learnings? Are there any biases that hinder your growth and understanding? Do your cherished values and beliefs face challenges that demand introspection? These inquiries, along with many others, unlock the door to a realm we call self-knowledge." Samantha nodded, her eyes shining with a newfound sense of purpose. She realized that self-knowledge was a multi-faceted journey, a quest to uncover the deepest truths about oneself.

In the mesmerizing encounter between the discussion team and their esteemed mentor, time seemed to slip away, paving the way for Guru Ji's final words. As the seekers gathered in the grand hall, eagerly awaiting the wisdom that would unfold, Guru Ji extended a warm welcome to all, his voice carrying an air of authority and grace.

"Dear seekers," he began, his tone both commanding and soothing, "I implore you to shift your perspective, to transcend the mere role of spectators. The question that echoes within each of us is 'Who Am I?' It is a question shrouded in complexity, for it encompasses the intricate interplay of body, mind, and soul—the very essence of our being."

With profound insight, Guru Ji continued, "As you keenly observe, read, and become acquainted with these three fundamental elements, you come to realize that you are more than the sum of their parts. They are but facets of a unified whole, wherein the body represents the tangible energy, the mind embodies subtlety, and the soul stands as the core essence."

In the realm of spiritualism, Guru Ji elucidated, "Self-knowledge stands as the ultimate culmination of all forms of knowledge. While knowledge may continuously evolve and transform, it is in the pursuit of self-discovery that we find the ultimate truth—an irrefutable reality that remains, unchallenged and undeniable, when all else fades away."

Within the grand theater of life, the soul revels in its dual role as both spectator and actor. It assumes the role of a spectator, simply observing and bearing witness to the intricate workings of the mind. And yet, it dons the garb of an actor, guiding the mind towards awareness and consciousness, immersing itself in the realm of duality where divine and devilish forces clash. Through the ever-changing roles of childhood, youth, middle age, and old age, the soul dances through life's stages, only to vanish and embark on a new game after the final curtain falls.

As the layers of existence are gradually peeled away, a profound emptiness is revealed, akin to the hollow core of an onion. In this nothingness, all illusions fade, leaving behind a vast expanse of pure essence. It is a state where energy itself is hailed as the ultimate truth. This power, indivisible and eternal, cannot be created nor destroyed; it possesses the remarkable ability to transform, evolve, expand, and reshape within its very essence.

Let me share a story to drive the point even deeper. In the enchanting realm of an ancient kingdom, a revered Zen master reaches a king's palace at late evening. The king, emanating regal authority, greeted the Zen master with humble intrigue, his voice resonating through the vast chamber. "How may I be of service to you?" inquired the king, eager to unravel the intentions of his nocturnal visitor.

Unveiling his wisdom with graceful eloquence, the Zen teacher gently revealed his humble request. "Oh, benevolent ruler, I humbly seek but a place to rest my weary soul for a solitary night. Would you kindly grant me refuge within the confines of this inn?" The king, captivated by the teacher's audacious proposition, chuckled heartily at the notion.

"Inn, you say? This resplendent palace, a mere inn?" laughed the king, his mirth reverberating through the air. The Zen master, undeterred by the king's mirthful response, posed a thought- provoking question, causing the regal laughter to dissipate like mist before the morning sun. “Is it truly your palace, O illustrious king? If that be so, please tell me, who graced these halls in times preceding your birth?” The king, momentarily taken aback by the teacher’s query, composed himself and replied, “My father, who has long departed this mortal realm, held dominion over this sacred abode before me.”

“And before your father, who dwelled within these resplendent walls?” questioned the teacher, his voice carrying the weight of ancient wisdom. The king, deep in contemplation, responded, “None other than my esteemed grandfather, whose spirit now resides in realms unknown.”

Pausing for a moment, the Zen teacher, his eyes gleaming with insight, delivered his illuminating verdict. “Dear king, it seems to me that this grand edifice serves as a dwelling for transient souls, who, in the cycle of existence, come and go like passing shadows. Could it not be, then, that this illustrious palace is, in truth, an inn?”

In the wake of these profound words, a paradigm shift washed over the king’s consciousness, as the realization of impermanence reverberated deep within his being. The notion of possessions, once deemed significant, now transformed into wisps of illusion. Boundless freedom, like a gentle breeze, caressed the core of his existence.

For the Zen teacher's wisdom had illuminated the truth—the ephemeral nature of life and the illusory quality of worldly belongings. Yet, this realization did not demand renunciation or withdrawal from the material realm. Instead, it urged an introspective journey, an inner realization of impermanence.

❑

7
Spirituality
Violet Spectrum

"You have to grow from the inside out. None can teach you; none can make you spiritual. There is no other teacher but your own soul"

- Swami Vivekananda

In the golden embrace of a breathtaking morning, Guru Ji extended his gracious welcome to the gathered multitude. Today, he declared with a resolute tone, our devotions shall transcend the boundaries of mere meditation. Instead, we shall embark on a profound prayer, one that encompasses every sentient being that graces the realms of this wondrous existence.

"Let our reverent entreaties cascade through the ether, traversing land, sea, and sky," Guru Ji implored, his voice carrying an ethereal cadence. "In unison, let us beseech for the sacred gifts of peace, harmony, joy, and an abundance of unadulterated bliss to grace the souls of all who walk, soar, or swim. May the essence of happiness permeate every nook and cranny of their lives."

With unwavering conviction, Guru Ji reminded his followers that the essence of their supplications was not confined to mere words, but lay instead in the purity and sincerity of their intentions. Such was the key to unlock the floodgates of benevolence without unsettling the equilibrium of others.

As their fervent prayers subsided, Guru Ji cast a tender gaze upon the assembly, his eyes brimming with a profound sense of purpose.

Today, he proclaimed, we shall embark upon the last vibrant hue of the spectral web— the mesmerizing hue of "Violet," a color that embodies the very essence of spirituality.

With utmost reverence, Guru Ji bowed before the multitude, paying homage to the myriad faiths that intertwined within their souls. "It is said with sagacity that religion serves as the gateway to the sacred temple of spirituality," he shared, his words carrying the weight of ancient wisdom. In this moment, he recognized the diverse paths that had guided each individual to this sacred gathering.

And thus, the purpose of this day unfurled before them like a blossoming lotus. Guru Ji sought to kindle a flame of awareness, igniting the embers of spirituality that lay dormant within their hearts. He understood that the web of spirituality was intricately woven into the fabric of their everyday lives, unique and personal to each soul.

With this revelation, Guru Ji unveiled a framework that would illuminate their collective journey. Through the enchantment of storytelling, he aimed to impart profound truths wrapped in the delicate embrace of anecdote. Tales of subtlety, depth, and wonder would lead them down the path of introspection, nurturing an awakening to the very core of their spiritual being.

In the hallowed presence of Guru Ji, a gentle breeze carried the murmurs of anticipation as he embarked on a tale close to his heart. A story whispered in the sacred corridors of his being, its essence yearning to touch the souls of those gathered.

Once, in a realm where kingdoms reigned and wisdom sought solace in the footsteps of a wandering monk, a king approached this illustrious sage. With reverence lacing his words, the king beseeched, "Master, can you guide me to the sublime encounter with God?" A flicker of a smile danced upon the monk's lips as he posed a question of his own, "Does your desire burn within you for an immediate meeting or can it be embraced in the passage of time?"

Perplexed, the king sought clarity. He clarified his reference to the supreme soul, the Almighty God. Understanding his intent, the monk gently nodded. "Indeed,

I am aware of whom you seek," he affirmed. Eagerly, the king expressed his longing to meet the divine presence without delay, should it be within the monk's power to orchestrate such a rendezvous.

With a sagacious aura, the monk's response was simple yet profound. "O King," he uttered, "may I request you to inscribe your name and address upon this parchment, that I may convey to God your existence?" The king, complying with the monk's request, diligently penned his name, his title, and the grand address of his opulent palace, presenting the document to the wise wanderer.

As the monk's eyes perused the written details, a quizzical expression danced upon his face. "But these, my dear king, are mere reflections," he gently intoned. Confusion clouded the king's countenance as he implored the monk to explain. "Consider this," the monk elucidated, "if your name were to change, would the essence of your being transform as well?" The king, recognizing the eternal truth in these words, replied, "Nay, for I am eternally myself, regardless of the labels that adorn me."

Undeterred, the monk continued his gentle inquiry. "And what if fate were to snatch your kingdom in the tempest of war? Who then, dear king, would emerge from the ashes of the fallen crown?" A flicker of understanding illuminated the king's eyes as he whispered, "Even in the absence of a kingdom or palace, I shall remain unaltered, unwavering in my essence."

Like a thunderbolt of realization, the truth struck the king's heart. In the depths of his being, he had lost sight of his true self. The monk's words resonated within him, echoing through the corridors of his consciousness. "Behold," the monk proclaimed, "if you do not fathom the depths of your own being, how can I introduce you to God? Seek first the discovery of your true self, for on that day, dear king, you shall no longer need my guidance to commune with the divine."

As the sun bathed the world in its warm embrace, Gopal Ji stood amidst his team, a beacon of welcoming light. A smile danced upon his lips, radiating a contagious enthusiasm that enveloped them all. Rahul, a seeker of knowledge, stepped forward, his eyes gleaming with curiosity. "Allow me to seek your wisdom, Gopal Ji," he humbly requested. "In my humble understanding, spirituality encompasses a profound connection to something greater than ourselves. It is a quest to uncover the elusive meaning that dwells within the various dimensions of life." Gopal Ji, nodding in agreement, acknowledged Rahul's perception. "Indeed," he responded, "your words capture the essence of spirituality beautifully."

Yet, Gopal Ji's countenance held a glimmer of intrigue, a spark of anticipation. "Dear Rahul," he continued, "while your grasp of spirituality is commendable, the voyage we embark upon today shall be imbued with even greater significance. It is within this realm that we unravel the answers to the two pillars of existence, the very foundation of our beings."

With bated breath, Rahul listened intently, his heart open to the wisdom about to be shared. Gopal Ji, his voice infused with gentle authority, imparted the truth that lay veiled in the mists of existence. "Consider, my dear friends, the profound questions that shape the fabric of our lives. Who am I? What is the purpose that ignites the flame of my existence?"

"For it is within the realm of self-discovery," Gopal Ji continued, "that we unearth the hidden treasures of spirituality. By embarking on this voyage, we shall unlock the doors to the profound mysteries that lie dormant within us, waiting to be awakened."

Eager to seize the moment, Samantha's hand rose gracefully, her heart brimming with a tale that yearned to be shared. "Allow me," she said, her voice filled with eager anticipation. "I bring to you the story of a parrot, a tale that holds the potential to touch the depths of our souls."

"Once, a person chanced upon a parrot, its vibrant plumage concealed within a golden cage," she began, her voice carrying the weight of empathy. "Within the confines of its gilded prison, the parrot murmured an incessant cry for freedom, as if its very essence longed to soar in boundless skies." The man, struck by the parrot's desire for liberation, resolved to become its savior. He decided to wait until darkness blanketed the world, for it was then that he would open the cage's doors and set the parrot free.

As the moon cast its gentle glow upon the scene, the man's hands cautiously opened the cage, his heart brimming with anticipation. To his astonishment, the parrot clung desperately to the bars, reluctant to embrace the freedom that beckoned. Perceiving the parrot's hesitation, the man believed it to be a lack of knowledge, a learned helplessness. Fueled by compassion, he attempted to cradle the parrot in his hands, ready to carry it to the skies.

Yet, the parrot resisted with all its might, its beak inflicting wounds upon the man's hand. Undeterred, the man persevered, his determination unwavering. Eventually, against all odds, he freed the bird from its confining cage. A sense of triumph washed over him, for he believed he had granted the parrot the coveted gift of freedom.

Settling into a night's rest, the man dreamt of a new day dawning, one where he would bask in the radiance of his benevolence. But as the morning sun stretched its golden rays across the world, a familiar cry reached the man's ears. "Freedom! Freedom!" echoed through the air, leaving him bewildered.

With a growing sense of curiosity, the man ventured forth, his eyes scanning the surroundings. And to his astonishment, he discovered the parrot once more within the cage, its doors wide open. Samantha paused, her voice heavy with contemplation, before sharing her personal connection to the tale that unfolded.

"In the depths of my being," she confided, her words resonating with authenticity, "I relate to this story on a profound level. It serves as a poignant reminder that true liberation stems from within, that sometimes the cages we find ourselves in are self-imposed. It is a call to reflect upon the barriers we construct, even when the doors to freedom stand ajar."

Within the sanctuary of their spiritual gathering, Rahul's fervent curiosity burst forth like a spark seeking illumination. "Gopal Ji," he inquired, his voice tinged with eagerness, "are there any discernible signs that indicate one's progress on the spiritual journey?"

Gopal Ji's countenance softened with a knowing smile, as if the secrets of the universe danced within his eyes. He reciprocated Rahul's enthusiasm with an air of gentle anticipation. "Let me weave a tale," he replied, his voice carrying the resonance of ancient wisdom. "In the realm of this story, you shall find the answer that has beckoned you."

Gopal Ji's narrative unfolded upon the canvas of their minds, transporting them to a tranquil countryside where two monks sought solace in their humble caves. People from far and wide sought their counsel, drawn to their profound wisdom and love that flowed effortlessly from their beings.

Yet, amidst the adoration they received, a stark contrast emerged between their dwelling places. One monk's abode glimmered with a resplendent golden glow, as if it held within its embrace a hidden source of radiance. The other monk's cave, however, lacked such ostentatious displays of luminosity. This divergence did not go unnoticed, and the seekers yearned for an understanding that eluded them.

Driven by their quest for enlightenment, they sought counsel from a sage, his eyes alight with the wisdom of ages. "Dear seekers," he began, his voice infused with tranquility, "as one embarks upon the path of self-discovery, various phenomena may manifest. Sounds, lights, and myriad other occurrences may grace their journey. However, it is vital not to perceive these as mere supernatural spectacles."

The sage's words settled like gentle dewdrops upon the listeners' souls, awakening a deeper understanding within. He cautioned against the fallacy of judgment, reminding them that the advancement of one's spiritual journey cannot be measured by external manifestations alone. Each monk traversed their unique path, evoking their own inner transformations, which remain concealed from the wandering eyes of external observers.

With newfound clarity, they embarked upon their own odysseys, their hearts aflame with the knowledge that the advancement of their spiritual journeys shall forever remain a sacred and intimate dance between themselves and the divine.

As the seekers gathered for the final words of Guru Ji, a radiant aura enveloped, reflecting the transformative nature of their shared journey. Guru Ji, ever perceptive, observed the serene expressions that graced their faces and commended them on completing the arduous odyssey of the seven-spectrum quest. A sense of accomplishment permeated the air, mingling with the anticipation of what lay ahead.

With a gentle cadence in his voice, Guru Ji addressed the assembled souls, his words weaving a curtain of wisdom that resonated with their spirits. "Tomorrow," he proclaimed, his eyes gleaming with purpose, "we shall draw this magnificent journey to a close, before the sun reaches its zenith."

Yet, for the present moment, Guru Ji yearned to leave them with a vivid scene, a tableau that would ignite their imaginations. "Imagine," he began, his voice carrying the weight of a master storyteller, "a rural road stretching ahead, a humble bullock cart slowly meandering upon its dusty path. Within its embrace, a farmer and his kin, journeying homeward after a day's toil." Guru Ji beckoned their attention to a peculiar sight—the presence of a dog, dutifully traversing the distance between the cart's wheels. And so, the story unfolded, revealing the dog's predicament, a call from nature disrupting his stride. Yet, with a selfless resolve, he chose to persevere, convinced that his momentary pause might hinder the farmer's progress.

Guru Ji's voice brimmed with gentle knowingness as he uttered the truth that resonated within their hearts. "In this journey of life," he explained, his words carrying a profound message, "we often find ourselves trapped within the illusion that the world around us will grind to a halt if we dare to pause. We believe that without our constant involvement, the very fabric of existence might unravel."

In the hushed stillness that followed, Guru Ji's words sank deep into the souls of his listeners, illuminating a path of understanding. With warmth and compassion, he urged them to embrace the beauty of life's pauses, to revel in the exquisite dance of moments where time stands still. "Dear friends," he whispered, his voice a gentle caress, "let not the fear of halting deter you from taking well-deserved breaks. For in these pauses, life unfolds its truest colors, granting depth and meaning to the journey."

Guru Ji's message settled within their beings, each listener assimilating the wisdom in their unique way. For it was in the celebration of life's pauses, the appreciation of the symphony that continued unabated, whether they were present or not, that the seekers found solace. Guru Ji reassured them, urging a delicate balance between detachment and immersion, a dance that honored both their individual growth and the purpose of existence.

❑

7 Pearl Club

"Balance is the key to everything. What we do, say, eat, feel, they all require awareness and through this awareness we can grow"

– Koi Fresco

The sunlit morning dawned, gracing the rainbow forest with a delicate drizzle as a congregation of souls converged upon the serene meditation hall. Guru Ji, a beacon of wisdom and tranquility, extended his warm greetings to the assembled seekers, their presence a testament to their willingness to carve out precious moments from their bustling lives. With an air of profound gratitude, he acknowledged the shared commitment of both himself and their mentors, emphasizing their divergence from the conventional paths of engineers and their deliberate choice not to mend tangible objects or enforce rigid doctrines.

Instead, their mission transcended the mundane, akin to shepherds guiding their flock, nurturing and gently guiding the tender spirits toward a captivating realm—the ethereal Rainbow Forest of ideas and concepts. Within this harmonious expanse, they believed resided the optimal convergence, a space where individuals hailing from diverse ethnic backgrounds and wielding contrasting perspectives could discover a shared sanctuary of introspection and self-revelation.

Allow me to introduce you to the illustrious Mr. David, a man of extraordinary vision and the brilliant mind behind the revered "7 Pearl Club." Having traversed this profound journey countless times, he emerges as the guiding light, spearheading the formation of this extraordinary collective. With utmost humility, I beseech Mr. David to grace us with his insights and unveil the enigmatic world of this remarkable club.

With a poised elegance, David rose from his seat, his hands folded in a gesture of reverence, and acknowledged the gathering before him. "I extend my deepest gratitude to each and every one of you," he spoke, his voice carrying a melodious timbre that resonated throughout the room. "And of course, my heartfelt appreciation goes to the esteemed Guru Ji for granting me this privilege of sharing my thoughts with you all."

David firmly believed in the age-old adage that "practice makes a man perfect." He expounded upon the notion that knowledge, if not nurtured and fortified through consistent application, tends to wane and fade amidst the ever-changing tides of life. It was during our collective voyage, as we embarked on our second expedition, that the seed of inspiration took root within our group. United by a shared realization, we recognized the necessity of coming together, setting aside a few precious hours each month to gather as the 7 Pearl Club. This sanctified space would serve as a haven where we could delve into the reservoir of each other's experiences, forging profound connections and providing solace during our moments of vulnerability.

Just as birds of the same feather instinctively flock together, we discovered unparalleled joy in soaring through life as a unified entity. The bonds we formed transcended the boundaries of birth and circumstance, gifting me with an abundance of brothers and sisters in this unfamiliar land. I extend to you an open invitation to become a cherished member of this esteemed club. Our manifold programs and offerings will be shared, allowing you to select and attend based on your availability. It is important to note that financial transactions hold no place within our hallowed sanctuary, as every contribution and participation is entirely voluntary. Our collective focus, you see, resides in the relentless pursuit of self-improvement—a ceaseless evolution toward becoming the finest versions of ourselves.

In that moment, as Rahul gazed upon David, a newfound understanding took root within his being. The veil of ambiguity lifted, revealing a profound clarity that resonated deep within his soul. Why had David beckoned him? The answer now seemed crystal clear.

Rahul's perception shifted, and a profound respect for David began to flourish within his heart. The realization washed over him like a gentle tide, whispering that there was much to be gleaned from this extraordinary individual. David's character exuded an ethereal grace, his humility a beacon that illuminated every interaction. Never once did he boast of his accomplishments, nor did he seek recognition for the wondrous achievement that was the club they had formed together.

With a commanding presence, Guru Ji gracefully assumed control of the gathering, his serene countenance emanating an aura of wisdom and tranquility. He invited the participants to step forward, encouraging them to share their reflections and offer any feedback for the dedicated organizing team who had orchestrated this transformative experience within the enchanting realm of Rainbow Forest.

One by one, individuals from diverse backgrounds and affiliations courageously stepped forward, their voices echoing with a profound resonance. And now, it was Gopal Ji's teams turn to impart their thoughts upon the attentive audience. Simon with heartfelt gratitude, extended his appreciation to Guru Ji, his mentor, and every soul who had played a role in making his stay within these hallowed grounds an unforgettable and meaningful sojourn. "I stand here today," he proclaimed, his voice ringing with conviction, "overflowing with pride, for I have invested these seven precious days, receiving the most invaluable gift of my existence."

Natasha, her spirit emboldened by the transformative energy of Rainbow Forest, chose her words with purpose. She remembered Guru Ji's metaphorical dog beneath a bullock cart, realizing that the world continued its relentless motion even in her absence. A profound truth had crystallized within her being—her team possessed the capacity to make decisions of utmost importance, guided by their own wisdom and with the best interests of the business at heart. Now, her personal quest lay in adding tangible value to the world, offering her unique contributions with unwavering dedication. And, with an unyielding determination, she vowed to move forward, leaving behind the weight of the past.

Samantha, moved by the depths of her self-introspection, found herself at a loss for words to adequately capture the profoundness of her learnings. She marveled at the rejuvenation that had blossomed within her during this remarkable journey. With humble gratitude, she articulated her belief that when one is truly prepared, the master will appear, guiding and illuminating the path ahead. This transformative odyssey had recalibrated her life's purpose, unveiling the delicate balance that imbued every facet of existence.

As Rahul embarked upon the profound journey of self-discovery, he found himself traversing the vast landscapes of his own being, only to stumble upon a realization that left him awestruck. Like a pendulum in perpetual motion, he discovered his existence oscillated between two or three distinct spectrums, their vibrations permeating his very essence. In some, his presence was but a mere whisper, a gentle brush of energy. In others, he found himself entirely absent, like a forgotten melody lost amidst the cacophony of life's symphony.

Yet, far from despondency, a radiant smile graced Rahul's lips, illuminating his countenance with newfound awareness. For within this epiphany lay the seeds of transformation and the potential for equilibrium. He reveled in the brilliance of his discovery, for it revealed a universal truth—life itself possessed an intricate dance of harmony and balance, a delicate interplay of energies and forces. And he understood, with every fiber of his being, that to unravel the enigma of existence, one must remain ever vigilant and consciously direct their efforts toward seeking the elusive equilibrium.

In this symphony of realization, Rahul embraced his newfound awareness, his heart brimming with contentment. The journey of self- discovery had gifted him with a precious understanding—that the key to a fulfilled and purposeful life lay in navigating the vast landscapes of balance, harmonizing the divergent aspects of his being.

With genuine appreciation, Guru Ji acknowledged Rahul's profound reflection, his words carrying the weight of wisdom and guidance. "Allow me to suggest," Guru Ji began, his voice filled with gentle authority, "that you cultivate a crystal-clear understanding of these seven spectrums within your mind's eye. At the end of each day, take a moment to evaluate your actions, to discern in which of these spectrums you were truly present. If not daily, then at least on a weekly basis."

He revealed a powerful tool that would serve as a compass on life's journey—an instrument of self-audit that would illuminate the path toward achieving one's deepest desires. Within the hallowed sanctuary of balance that we all seek, Guru Ji emphasized the paramount importance of objectivity in our evaluations. By employing this introspective lens, you would unearth the truth of your own existence, discovering that the normal routines often confined us to a few spectrums. And thus, we would embark upon a deliberate quest, seeking out activities and endeavors that would allow us to explore the uncharted territories of the other spectrums.

Guru Ji's conviction was unwavering as he assured the gathered souls, "Trust me, if you approach this task with unwavering diligence, your life will undergo a transformation of the most profound nature. Every facet, be it personal or professional, will take on a newfound meaning and purpose." The promise of a life imbued with deep significance hung in the air, tantalizingly within reach.

In a world brimming with celestial equilibrium, Guru Ji implored his listeners to contemplate a vital question—why did they, in their unique existence, find themselves out of balance? The knowledge and exposure they had gained in their journey thus far would serve as the foundation for their transformation, but it was in the application of these insights that true metamorphosis would occur. Trusting in the benevolence of the divine forces that governed the universe, they would be bestowed with wisdom at every stage of their evolution.

And so, with heartfelt sincerity, Guru Ji bestowed upon them his final words, a benediction of sorts. "May you all find the elusive embrace of balance, not only within yourselves but also in the interactions you share with others. May your lives radiate harmony and purpose, becoming a testament to the infinite possibilities that lie within the pursuit of equilibrium." The stage was set, and the journey that lay ahead promised not only personal transformation but a profound ripple effect that would touch the lives of all they encountered.

❑

Rahul & Chairman

"Transformation in the world happens when people are healed and start investing in other people"

– Michael W. Smith

As Rahul stepped through the threshold of his home, a sense of anticipation hung in the air. Seema and Ayesha, his wife and daughter, awaited his return with bated breath, eager to witness the transformation that had graced his being. And there it was, etched upon his countenance—a serene grace, a tranquil peace that radiated from within.

With genuine curiosity, Seema and Ayesha inquired about Rahul's sojourn, their eyes locked onto him as they sought to unravel the enigma of his experience. And in that moment, Rahul's words flowed forth, tinged with a profound sense of wonder. "It was beyond words," he confessed, his voice carrying the weight of a newfound understanding. "I forged new connections, forming friendships that breathed life into my journey. And after each session, I found myself blessed with ample time for introspection, a respite from the clutches of screens and external distractions."

He chuckled softly, reminiscing on the initial moments of his retreat, when boredom threatened to cloud his days. But as time unfolded, a beautiful transformation took place within him. "I discovered the joy of solitude, of embracing my own company," Rahul shared with unreserved honesty. "In those quiet moments, thoughts of both of you filled my heart more intensely than they ever did when I was physically present. It is a confession, raw and true."

Seema and Ayesha exchanged glances, their eyes sparkling with amazement. As Rahul's words danced upon their ears, they realized they were conversing with a man reborn—an individual touched by a profound awakening. The aura that surrounded him was laced with newfound purpose, radiating a warmth and depth that transcended their wildest expectations.

In the comforting embrace of their home, Seema revealed a remarkable occurrence to Rahul—one that stirred a sense of intrigue and anticipation. She shared that the Chairman's secretary had graced their abode just a week prior, her purpose twofold: to seek an audience with Rahul and to convey the Chairman's heartfelt desire to meet him. A bouquet of vibrant flowers had accompanied her, an offering that carried the weight of importance.

Rahul, upon hearing this news, absorbed the information with a calm resolve. "Tomorrow," he affirmed, his voice carrying a tone of assurance. "I shall honor the Chairman's request and meet him." His words held a quiet determination, for he understood that this meeting held significance, a purpose yet to be unveiled.

Curiosity danced in Seema's eyes as she posed the inevitable question: "Why does the Chairman wish to see you? What could be the reason?" The weight of uncertainty pressed upon her, and yet, Rahul's response caressed her concerns with a soothing reassurance.

"Relax," he urged, his voice gentle and soothing. "Not everything needs immediate answers. Just as the grandness of life unfurls, we find ourselves gracefully swaying to the rhythm of a divine melody. Trust that everything unfolds in its own time, guided by a purpose that may reveal itself in due course."

Rahul, adorned in a cloak of anticipation, arrived at the hallowed grounds of the Chairman's office, punctual and resolute. As he stepped into the room, the Chairman stood there, a beacon of authority, his arms outstretched in a heartfelt embrace—a gesture that caught Rahul by surprise. Breaking the silence, the Chairman's voice resonated with a mix of sincerity and candor. "Rahul," he began, his words carrying the weight of wisdom, "when you tendered your resignation, I accepted it, for I did not wish to dampen your spirits in anticipation of an award."

With a gentle nod, they made their way into the inner sanctum—a meeting room adorned with the presence of other board members.

The air crackled with intrigue as they took their seats, the collective gaze of the room falling upon Rahul. The Chairman's voice pierced the stillness, his words laden with curiosity and a desire for clarity. "We withheld the announcement of your resignation, Rahul, for we sought to understand your plans, your vision for the future of our esteemed organization. Your insights hold immense value, and we stand here, ready to listen and to forge a path of transformation."

With an unwavering composure, Rahul stood tall, his voice infused with the wisdom garnered from his transformative journey. Before the discerning eyes of the board, he acknowledged the profound insights he had gained in the realm of balance—an exquisite blend of art and science. It was this realization that had illuminated the path before him, exposing the areas in which he needed to grow and evolve.

A deep sense of gratitude welled within Rahul as he addressed the board, expressing his appreciation for their trust and the opportunity to share his perspective. In a display of vulnerability, he admitted that there were aspects of his own being that required attention and refinement—a commitment to becoming a better, more complete version of himself.

With humility as his guiding light, Rahul offered his insights and unwavering support to the incoming CEO, advocating for the selection of an internal candidate. The Chairman, ever attentive, posed a question that danced upon the precipice of Rahul's purpose within the organization. Pausing briefly, he crafted his response—a vision steeped in mentorship and growth, a desire to propel the team beyond the boundaries of their current horizons while simultaneously nurturing his own continuous learning.

Rahul's gaze turned inward, his voice resolute as he unveiled his grand vision for Media Global—an entity in need of recalibration, an organization poised to embrace a new dawn. Relationships, he proclaimed, would serve as the cornerstone of their future endeavors. Empathy, he believed, must flow through the very core of their collective actions. Gone were the days of measuring success solely through materialistic pursuits. Instead, Rahul championed a paradigm shift—an all-encompassing definition of success that accounted for the far-reaching consequences of their efforts.

In his newfound wisdom, Rahul placed utmost importance on weaving a fabric of meaningful connections, both within the organization and with their esteemed clients. It was from this foundation of empathy and purpose that true sustainability would flourish. With unwavering conviction, Rahul implored Media Global to transcend the boundaries of the conventional, to embrace a multidimensional approach that resonated with the very essence of their existence.

The board members sat in awe; their eyes transfixed upon Rahul as his words cascaded like pearls of wisdom from his lips. In that moment, he transformed before their very eyes—a figure of profound insight, embodying the essence of a true thought leader. Yet, despite his newfound stature, he remained grounded, his humility shining through every word he uttered.

The Chairman, his voice resonating with pride and admiration, addressed Rahul with a warmth that enveloped the room. "Rahul," he declared, his words carrying the weight of the collective sentiment, "we stand here, proud of the person you have become, and eager to witness the contributions you shall bring to our beloved company." The unanimous agreement reverberated through the air as they embraced Rahul's proposal, entrusting him with the pivotal responsibility of seeking out the new CEO. With a chorus of well wishes, they bestowed upon him their utmost support, a collective blessing for his newfound role as Chief Mentor.

In that sacred space of transition, the Chairman's words echoed with a sense of curiosity and anticipation. He implored Rahul to share the invaluable lessons he had gleaned from his time in the mystical realm of the rainbow forest—an invitation extended to all board members, their hearts yearning for the wisdom that Rahul possessed. For in his transformative journey, he had become a beacon of knowledge, a guide from whom they too wished to learn.

As the words lingered in the air, a blend of gratitude wove its way through the room. Rahul, now entrusted with a profound task and recognized as a beacon of wisdom, stood tall, his heart overflowing with a renewed sense of purpose. The chapters of his life continued to unfold, revealing new adventures and challenges that awaited him on the path to come.

❑